SRI RAMANUJACHARYA

SRI RAMANUJACHARYA

A SKETCH OF

HIS LIFE AND TIMES

BY

S. KRISHNASWAMI AIYANGAR, M.A.

HIS PHILOSOPHICAL SYSTEM

BY

T. RAJAGOPALA CHARIAR, M.A., B.L.

WITH AN ACCOUNT OF

RAMANUJA AND VAISHNAVISM

BY

RAO BAHADUR PROF. M. RANGACHARYA

GYAN

Published by

GYAN

Gyan Publishing House
5, Ansari Road
Daryaganj, New Delhi-110002
Phone: 011-47034999, 9811692060
E-mail: books@gyanbooks.com

Distribution Network
gyanbooks.com
India, USA, Canada, UK, Australia

ISBN: 978-93-6280-445-7 (PB)
First Published, 1911

2nd Impression 2024

Printed at: Gyan Press, Delhi.

SRI RAMANUJACHARYA
Author: S. KRISHNASWAMI AIYANGAR, T. RAJAGOPALA CHARIAR, RAO BAHADUR PROF. M. RANGACHARYA

SRI RAMANUJACHARYA

A SKETCH OF

HIS LIFE AND TIMES

BY

S. KRISHNASWAMI AIYANGAR, M.A.

HIS PHILOSOPHICAL SYSTEM

BY

T. RAJAGOPALA CHARIAR, M.A., B.L.

WITH AN ACCOUNT OF

RAMANUJA AND VAISHNAVISM

BY

RAO BAHADUR PROF. M. RANGACHARYA

CONTENTS.

Sri Ramanujacharya

HIS LIFE AND TIMES

BY

MR. S. KRISHNASWAMI AIYANGAR, M.A., M.R.A.S.

GENERAL CHARACTER OF SOUTH INDIAN HISTORY.

TO the religious history of India, the contributions that the Southern half has had to make have been many. The South generally enjoyed more peaceful development and was long out of the convulsions that threw the North into confusion, and all the internal revolutions and external attacks sent out the pulse of the impact almost spent out to the South. This has been of great advantage and it is precisely in the dark ages of the North, that often intervened brighter epochs, that the South sent out its light to redeem the darkness.

SOUTH INDIAN CONTRIBUTION TO RELIGIONS IN INDIA.

This general character of the history of the North of India from the first centuries of the Christian era onwards makes a continuous history impossible on certain lines; while in the South during this period, there has been a continuity of development amidst all the din and clang of war and dynastic revolutions. Our concern here is about the Vaishnava movement and this has had a continuous history almost from the beginning of the Christian era.

MIS-IMPRESSIONS REGARDING RAMANUJA.

There has been considerable mis-impression that the Vaishnava movement originated in Ramanuja and all those that claim to be Vaishnavas (not including the disciples of Madhwa who are Vaishnava in a narrower sense) both in the North and the South can trace their particular form of Vedanta no earlier than Ramanuja. On the basis of this mis-impression, theories have been built up time and again that the characteristic features of the special teachings of Ramanuja have been borrowed from Christianity. The latest exponent of this theory is Dr. Grieson, though he would make a considerable distinction between the Vaishnavas of modern times and those of the older, and perhaps, set those of the North against the South. This no doubt is an error which arises from not giving due weight to the indebtedness of Ramanuja to those Tamil saints that had gone before him long ere he came into the world. The hypothesis would be untenable unless it could be proved that all these Tamil saints could be shown also to have visited the Christian shrine at Mylapore or elsewhere. Besides, even from the point of view of Sanskrit Vaishnavaism, it cannot be said to have been proven that the peculiar features of Ramanuja-Vaishnavaism is not traceable to earlier works and teachers. Hence a life of Ramanuja based on historical material alone and free from the legends that have gathered round it, as time wore off, would be of great advantage to clear away the wrong impressions that prevail regarding his life and teaching.

THE SPECIAL PERIOD OF RAMANUJA'S ADVENT.

That Ramanuja should have appeared in the eleventh century is quite as much of the mission getting the man as the advent of the Buddha in the sixth century before Christ. This century in the south of India was characterised by considerable religious ferment. It was then that each religious sect among the people felt the need for formulating a creed of its own and placing itself in a regularly organised religious body so as to be able to hold its own in the midst of the disintegrating influences that gained dominance in society. That Ramanuja appeared and did what is ascribed to him is just in the fitness of things, having regard to the circumstances of the times.

PREDECESSORS OF RAMANUJA.

(*a*) THE ALVARS.

There have been a succession of devotees called in Vaishnava parlance Alvars in contradistinction to a similar Saiva group called Adiyars. These two classes had considerable similarity with characteristic distinctions. They both laid stress on the doctrine of Bhakti as a means to the attainment of salvation, the one through Vishnu and the other through Siva. The Vaishnava tradition names twelve of the Alvars while the Saiva saints number sixty-three. The Tamil works of the former including a centum upon Ramanuja himself, constitute the Prabhandum 4,000, while those of the Saivas constitute a vaster collection of Tevarams, &c.

The twelve Alvars are in the traditional order:

I	1.	Poygai Alvar.
	2.	Bhutathu Alvar.
	3.	Pey Alvar.
II	4.	Tirumalisai Alvar.
III	5.	Nammalvar.
	6.	Madhurakavi Alvar.
IV	7.	Kulasekharalvar.
V	8.	Periyalvar.
	9.	Andal.
VI	10.	Tindaradippodi Alvar.
	11.	Tiruppanalvar.
	12.	Tirumangai Alvar.

The actual dates ascribed by the hagiologists to these Alvars would not bear scrutiny, but the order in which they are mentioned is substantially correct. In order of importance, Nammalvar stands first, and it is his work that has the distinctive appellation Tiruvoymoli —"the word of the mouth." They were all regarded by the generations that succeeded them, as manifestations of divine wisdom to redeem the world from the rilous plights to which it had brought itself.

(*b*) THE ACHARYAS.

The next group that followed, as the hagiologists would have us believe, in unbroken succession, is known as Acharyas (or preceptors) not so near to the divine, but still raised above the ordinary man of the world by much. This orthodox successions of apostles include six names before Ramanuja, of which the two most important are Nathamuni and his grand-son.

Alavandar. The great grand-son of this latter through one of his grand-daughters was Ramanuja.

PARENTAGE AND BIRTH OF RAMANUJA.

While Alavandar was still in occupation of the apostolic seat of the Vaishnavas at Srirangam, one of his grandsons requested permission of him to go and devote himself to the service of God on the Tirupathi Hill. The permission was graciously accorded and the young man went and settled there with his venerable father and two younger sisters. While there, two young men wishing to enter life as house-holders happened to go to the holy place and sought each the hand of one of the sisters. Of these two Asuri Kesava Bhattar of Sri Perumbuthur wedded the elder, while Kamalnayana Bhattar of Malalaimangalam accepted the younger of the girls. Of the first pair in course of time was born a boy (in 1017 A. D.) whom the maternal uncle named Lakshmana (otherwise Ramanuja or in Tamil, Ilaya Perumal.)

EARLY LIFE OF RAMANUJA.

Of the childhood of Ramanuja, as of others in similar positions of life, very little is known. There appears to have been nothing extraordinary in his career except that he appears to have lost his father while young. He received the kind of education ordinarily given to boys of his class and age along with his cousin, (mother's sister's son) Govinda Bhattar, as he was called. The two young men had advanced sufficiently to seek a teacher in the Vedanta to instruct them. They went to a teacher of reputation holding his classes in Conjeevaram and this change marks the turning point in the career of the young men.

RAMANUJA AND YADAVAPRAKASA.

Under Yadavaprakasa then the two cousins Ramanuja and Govina Bhattar were both studying the Vedanta assiduously. The former made such progress and his great-grandfather at Srirangam had heard such good reports of his remarkable advance, that he travelled all the way *incognito* to see the young man. This he did in the Deva Raja Shrine at Conjeevaram. Gratified with the look of the young man, he went back hoping that he might soon transfer the mantle of office to the youth of great promise that he just saw. He did not wish to speak to Ramanuja lest it should attract attention and disturb Ramanuja's studies in any way. Ramanuja went on with his studies yet a while, when he began to feel that at times Yadavaprakasa's interpretations of Vedic passages were not quite up to his satisfaction. On one occasion, he even went the length of offering an explanation of his own which struck those about, as more satisfactory than that of his master. This led to grave differences between master and disciple. Matters advanced a step further when at the invitation of the ruler of the place, Yadavaprakasa failed in an attempt at exorcising. The princess was possessed and the spirit declined to move at Yadava's bidding. It would, however, go away if it were Ramanuja's pleasure that it should. Ramanuja was pleased to give the order and the ghost was raised. This made Yadava more jealous of his pupil and the crisis was reached when interpreting another Upanishad; Yadava again rendered the passage in a somewhat absurdly disrespectful manner. Ramanuja showed positive disapproval of what he considered a purposeful distortion of the texts. Yadavaprakasa asked Ramanuja to leave his academy, but was advised to get rid of Ramanuja altogether.

ATTEMPT AT ASSASSINATION OF RAMANUJA.

At the instigation of some of his disciples Yadava organised a pilgrimage to Benares, and Ramanuja and his cousin were among the party. The latter having been more docile stood in high favour with the master and was in the secrets of the plot to assassinate Ramanuja. It was arranged to kill him in the depths of the forests, perhaps not very far from Kanchi. Information of this was given to Ramanuja in time and he escaped at dead of night, and journeyed back to Kanchi under the guidance of a kind hunter and huntress. At daybreak the latter asked for a little water and when Ramanuja got down a well to fetch her some, the pair disappeared. Ramanuja had not to travel much farther before he came in sight of the spires of the great tmeple at Kanchi.

RAMANUJA'S RETURN AFTER ESCAPE.

Having reached Kanchi and intimated to his mother of what had happened and how he escaped death by divine intervention, he settled down as a householder at the instance of his mother, and devoted himself to the service of God Devaraja at Kanchi. Alavandar was drawing near his end in the meanwhile, and those about him despatched the eldest among his disciples to go and bring Ramanuja to Srirangam. Periyanambi, as this emissary was called, arrived at Kanchi and stood reciting one of the beautiful verses in praise of God (the Stotraratna) composed by his master Alavandar. Ramanuja's attention was drawn to the slokas (verses) in spite of his single-minded devotion to his preparation for the morning service. Turning round he asked the stranger who the composer of the piece was. Periyanambi answered it was his great master Alavandar. The next question was necessarily, whether he could see him. "If you would go with me now," said Periyanambi, "I will take you to him." Ramanuja hurried through his morning service and started with Periyanambi, having obtained permission of Devaraja for the journey.

RAMANUJA'S FIRST JOURNEY TO SRIRANGAM TO VISIT ALAVANDAR.

They journeyed along till they reached the northern side of Srirangam when at a distance Ramanuja descried a group of men on the south bank of the Koleroon River. Approaching closer Periyanambi and his younger companion discovered that Alavandar was no more and the group consisted of his disciples, came there with the remains of the departed great one for its final disposal. Remanuja was taken close to the body to take a first and final look at the great master, when lo! he saw three out of the five fingers of the right hand folded. Struck with this, he enquired whether the effect was noticed in life and the answer came that the defect was not physical and was not noticed in life. On further enquiry Ramanuja was told that the master had three of his cherished objects unfulfilled, namely, an easily-read and understood commentary upon the Brahmasutra; the giving of the names of Parasara and Shadagopa to suitable persons that would make these names live among the people. Ramanuja promised to see these fulfilled and the fingers straightened. Ramanuja waited for the funeral ceremonies to be completed and returned to Kanchi to resume his duties of devotion to God.

RETURN OF RAMANUJA TO KANCHI AND THE MISSSON OF HIS FUTURE.

Days having passed, in his usual round of service Ramanuja feft that time was passing without any attempt on his part to perform what he had promised to do. Not knowing what exactly to do, he appealed to the elderly priest of God Devaraja and wished that he might ascertain the divine will regarding his own future. Tirukkachchinambi as the priest was called, gave out the will of God, in the matter, in the following sloka:

"Sreman param tatvam aham, matam me bhedaha, prapattirnirapaya hetuhu,

Navasyakicha smriti, hiantyakale mokshaha, mahapurnaha iha aryavaryaha."

"I am the supreme, my conviction is distinction, devotion is the unfailing cause of salvation, conscious volition not essential, release in the end; at present Periyanambi is the highest preceptor."

In these six phrases was Ramanuja given the direction for his future work, whether the actual direction came from within himself or from without or those about. He was to pin his faith to God and work out the qualified monastic system of Indian philosophy accepting Periyanambi for his initiation, and teaching the doctrines of devotion to God whose self-imposed duty it is to give salvation even without the conscious volition of the person wishing it. Ramanuja felt the call and with the permission of Devaraja, accorded through his priest, he started towards Srirangam.

RAMANUJA'S INITIATION UNDER PERIYANAMBI.

He halted at Madhurantakam to pay his homage of worship to the God Rama in the temple there on the tank bund; and while in the act, he saw Periyanambi who was on his way to Kanchi. They both enquired of each other the puropse of his journey and found that each had in a way come to the end of it. Ramanuja found the Guru (preceptor) he sought, while Periyanambi's object was to take Ramanuja to Srirangam. In fact he had been sent on that special mission by the disciples of first degree of the late master Alavandar. At Ramanuja's importunate entreaty Nambi initiated him into the mysteries of the hidden lore of the Vedanta of those times, in presence of God Rama in the temple. Both Nambi and Ramanuja returned to Kanchi; master and disciple together lived there for some time. But their separation came soon and gave a turn to the whole career of Ramanuja.

CIRCUMSTANCES LEADING TO RAMANUJA'S RENUNCIATION.

Nambi and Ramanuja took up lodgings together and the two families were living amicably together for some time. Ramanuja, however, does not appear to have been very happy in the choice of his wife. He did not find in her that ready sympathy and compliance to his own wishes he expected of her. On one occasion he had invited Tirukachchinambi to his hous and the two were seated and conversed together for a while. When the former went away Ramanuja's wife quickly washed the seat occupied by him, the temple-priest having been of a slightly inferior status in point of caste. Ramanuja felt agrieved and overlooked this offence with an admonition. Again one morning while he was still by the accustomed well preparing for the morning service at the temple, a poor man asked him for food. He directed him home with instructions to demand food of Ramanuja's wife with the husband's permission. She said there was none available. The man returned intimating Ramanuja of how he fared. Ramanuja's enquiry on returning home proved that there was some food which might have been given to the person. Again he excused her. But the third offence proved the last straw, and was the most serious of all in Ramanuja's estimation. Ramanuja's wife and Periyanambi's both of them went to the same well to fetch water. It would appear that through the latter's carelessness some water from her vessel dropped into that of the other. This naturally led to some altercation in which the relative claims of the two families were rather too freely discussed by Ramanuja's wife. The other lady reported the matter to her husband, who rather than offend the good man quitely broke up establishment and returned to Srirangam.

RAMANUJA'S RENUNCIATION.

Ramanuja soon found out the cause of Nambi's unceremonious departure and resolved that the time had come for separating from his wife. He took advantage of an invitation from his father-in-law to send his wife away and without further delay assumed the brown robes of a *sannyasi* (he that has renounced the world). This step at once added to the rising reputation of Ramanuja, and disciples began to gather round him. It was now that disciples first appear round Yathiraja (king of hermits,) as he came to be called. It was probably now also that the question assumed importance whether a *sannyasi* should be of the Ekadandi or Tridandi (single rod or triple rod, as the symbol of office). The Vaishnava version has it that Yadavaprakasa, his late master, became a convert to Ramanuja under the name, Govindayogi and wrote the work *Yatidharma Samuchchayam.* (The enquiry into the rules of conduct of a hermit.)

RAMANUJA SETTLES DOWN AT SRIRANGAM AND PREPARES HIMSELF TO FULLFIL HIS MISSION.

While Ramanuja was making progress in this manner the disciples of Alavandar at Srirangam wished to get him to live in their midst, and occupy the seat of their late master which had remained unoccupied for lack of a suitable successor. This time they sent another of Alavandar's immediate disciples, his own son, by name Tiruvarangapperumal Ariyar. Ramanuja followed the Ariyar and settled down at Srirangam. It was now that he set about seriously to acquire the qualifications which alone would justify his accession to the high position to which he was looked upon by the public as the most worthy candidate. He had, therefore, to get himself initiated in every department of learning and philosophy which then constituted the Vaishnava lore. Periyanambi having become his *guru* (preceptor) in one part, he had to seek initiation of Tirukottiyurnambi for another (manthrartham). He went six times in succession and on all these occasions the master was not satisfied with the earnestness of the disciple and declined to open his mind. Ramanuja in despondency thought of giving up the business when he was asked to try another time. He succeeded in inducing the great one to unlock his secrets, after the customary promise not to publish except to a worthy disciple previously tried. Ramanuja agreed and found the secrets of such efficacy for salvation that he taught all about him what he learnt. The guru summoned the disciple to his presence and asked him how it was that he so flagrantly transgressed the injunctions of his master. Ramanuja begged to be prescribed the punishment and the *guru* replied that the punishment would be 'eternal hell' hereafter, but nothing here, Ramanuja replied:

with characteristic beneficence that he would gladly suffer 'hell' himself, if by so doing he was instrumental in ministering to the attainment of salvation to the suffering millions of humanity. The master appreciated the spirit of the disciple's transgression and said that the particular *darsana* (section of Vedanta) might hereafter be known 'Ramanuja darsana.'

CONVERSION OF RAMANUJA'S COUSIN.

At this period Ramanuja had to intervene in the affairs of his cousin and companion at school, Govinda Bhattar. This young man had continued his journey along with Yadavaprakasa to the Ganges. It would appear that while he bathed in the holy waters of the river, a 'phallic emblem' struck to the palm of his hand. Hence the name Ullangai Gonarndanayanar. Ever since, he had become a staunch Saivite and had taken residence at Kalahasti not far from his maternal uncle at Tirupathi. At Ramanuja's request the uncle met the nephew and brought him back to allegiance to the Vaishnava persuasion under the new sacerdotal designation of Embar. Ramanuja's name had begun to attract attention and he felt that he should still acquire other qualifications before becoming every way the head of a 'darsana.'

RAMANUJA COMPLETES HIS QUALIFICATIONS.

He began his studies in Tiruvoymoli first under Tiruvarangapperumal Ariyar and then under Tirumalaiyandan. While with the latter, he had occasion to show his special acuteness of intellect in suggesting special interpretations of important texts, which on further discussions were found to have been in full agreement with the views of Alavandar. This new acquisition completed his round of qualifications and he had become in fact a successor of Alavandar in every sense of the term.

A SECOND ATTEMPT ON RAMANUJA'S LIFE.

Ramanuja's fame had spread so wide and he came to be known so well that his little cousin at Tirupathi (son of his maternal uncle) evinced a precocious desire to attach himself to Ramanuja. The father sent the boy in charge of a nephew of his own and the two arrived at Srirangam when Ramanuja's life had been saved by the unlooked for intervention of a good woman. Ramanuja, as a *sannyasi* had to go round at mid-day from house to house for food. One of the householders had instructed his wife to poison the food and serve it to him. The woman felt compelled to obey the husband, but on giving the handful to Ramanuja, could not bear the feeling that the good man would die of the food. She, therefore, prostrated before him while getting back into the house. It is recognised as a rule of practice that when a *sannyasi* goes out for alms (biksha), no one should make the usual salutation. This strange conduct on the part of the lady struck Ramanuja and he suspected foul play. On examination the poisoning was discovered and ever after it was arranged that the elder of the two new arrivals should under take the food-supply of Ramanuja. In spite of this attempt at assassination, all had so far gone smoothly; and the life of Ramanuja becomes stormy hereafter. His fame had spread far and the few prominent conversions attracted attention. Whether he wished it or no, he had to make his position good against all comers and had to assume the role of a controversialist.

CONTROVERSY WITH YEGNAMURTI.

At this time there arrived at Srirangam an advaitic *sannyasi* by name Yegnamurti, in the course of a controversial tour through India. There began between the two a great disputation regarding the relative superiority of their respective creeds. For sixteen days they went on with no decisive result either way and Ramanuja was somewhat anxious about his own position, when it struck him that he might derive some help from Alavandar's works. He referred to the latter's Mayavadakandanam (a refutation of the idealistic theory.) Thus armed he overcame his adversary on the seventeenth day and as a result, enlisted his rival among his followers under the Vaishnava designation of Arulalapperumal Emberumanar.

RAMANUJA'S FULFILMENT OF HIS FIRST PROMISE.

Sometime after Ramanuja felt that he might conveniently pay the long wished-for visit to his uncle, who sent word through his nephew that he very much wished to see him. Ramanuja then set forward to Tirupathi, one of the three 'holy of holies' of the Sri Vaishnavas. He stayed there a year receiving instruction in the Ramayana from his maternal uncle there, who at the end of the period made over to him his two sons. His preparations were now complete and as he was growing old, he set about fulfilling his undertaking to Alavandar. The first of his three promises was the writing out of such a commentary for the Brahmasutra as would embody the views of the qualified monistic school of thought. It was absolutely essential for a due performance of this work that he should acquaint himself with the previous commentators, particularly of the Bodhayanavritti. This naturally was not easy of acquisition for one of his intentions explicit and implied. He had to go about much before he found access to a library in the North, containing the work, where he was allowed just to read it through. He felt that it was not enough when a quick disciple among his followers came to his rescue by saying that he had completely mastered the work and could give references whenever wanted. This was one among his first disciples, who lived to render yet greater services to his master. With the help of Kurathalvar—for such was the name of this stout-hearted and quick-minded disciple Ramanuja wrote out the three works, the essence of the Vedanta (Vedantasaram), a resume of the Vedanta (Vedanta Sangraham), the light of the Vedanta (Vedantadipam). He also wrote, or rather gave out, the commentaries on the Brahmasutra and Bhagavatgita. This list of works redeemed Ramanuja from his first promise.

RAMANUJA SECURES THE APPROVAL OF THE LEARNED FOR HIS BHASHYA.

But these must be accepted before Ramanuja could feel he had done his duty to his master. He had, therefore, to start on a tour to different places to secure the approval of the learned. This tour naturally took him to the great seat of learning, Kashmir. There at Sarasvatipita (the seat of learning) he read through the work in an assembly of philosophers and obtained from them the approval of no less an authority than "Sarasvati" herself. As a token of her approval she presented Ramanuja with the image of Hayagriva (horse-necked, an aspect of Vishnu) and said that his commentary might thereafter be known Sri Bhashya (*the* commentary). It is because of this distinction that among his disciples Ramanuja is known Bhashyakarar (maker of the Bhashya). The image of Hayagriva has come down to the present generation and is believed to be that which is the object of worship at the Parakalamutt at Mysore.

RAMANUJA SETTLES SAIVA-VAISHNAVA DISPUTE AT TIRUPATHI.

Returning from the North he had to pass by way of Tirupathi where matters had assumed a serious aspect on a dispute as to the nature of the deity there. The Saivas claimed the shrine to be that of God Subrahmaniya while the Vaishnavas claimed it as that of Vishnu. The matter had, therefore, to be settled one way or the other and they agreed to leave the decision to the God himself. It was arranged that one evening both parties should assemble and lock up the *sanctum sanctorum* having placed the weapons peculiar to each deity. The shrine was to be that of Vishnu or Siva according as the one set or the other was assumed by God. It was found the next morning that the image had assumed the disc and conch characteristic of Vishnu, and ever after the shrine appears to have been taken to be that of Vishnu. Having settled this dispute Ramanuja returned to Srirangam and set about arranging matters for getting through the remaining items of work he had undertaken.

RAMANUJA FULFILS THE SECOND DESIDERATUM.

SAHASRANAMA BHASHYA.

Ramanuja's foremost disciple Kurathalvar was for long childless. One night it would appear he had to go to bed without food having had to fast the whole day for lack of provisions. The bell in the great temple pealed indicating that the night-worship was going on. The devoted wife thought to herself that it was hardly fair that God Ranganatha should accept regular worship when the staunchest of his devotees lay starving. Soon after the temple priests brought a supply of food from the temple and knocked at the door of Kurathalvar. The wife opened the door and delighted with the arrival of food, woke up the restless husband and fed him. As the direct outcome of this divine favour, she soon became mother of two sons to one of whom at the instance of Ramanuja, the name Parasara was given. This boy had grown up to man's state when Ramanuja was looking out for some one through whom he might fulfil the second object. This young man Parasara Bhatta was commissioned to write a commentary on the *Sahasranama* (the thousand *names of Vishnu). This work of Parasara Bhatta* fulfilled the second of the desiderata of Alavandar.

PILLAN'S 6000 COMMENTARY ON THE TIRUVOYMOLI.

FULFILMENT OF THE THIRD DESIDERATUM.

There then remained the means of perpetuating the name of Nammalvar, the author of the Tiruvoymoli. Ramanuja was perhaps thinking of a commentary himself. It would appear he was contemplating within a closed room a particular verse of the work attempting to realize its full significance when his cousin looked through a chink in the door. The young man, Pillan by name, forthwith put the question whether the master was pondering the verse referring to the God at Tirumalirunjola. Ramanuja was struck with the acuteness of the young man, and commissioned him to write out the 6000 commentary on the Tiruvoymoli, giving him the name Tirukkuruhaippiran Pillan, the first part of which being one of the many surnames of Nammalvar. This brought the third of Alavandar's desiderata to fulfilment. Ramanuja could now feel his mission at an end and settle down to a life of quiet teaching. This way perhaps years rolled by.

THE CHOLA PERSECUTION AND ESCAPE OF RAMANUJA.

He was not, however, altogether unmolested. Perhaps a change of ruler or a change in his surroundings brought about a change in the spirit of complete tolerance that as a rule characterised the administration. Be the cause what it may, the Chola ruler for the time being, often given the name Kulothunga, took it into his head to demand assent to the doctrine,

"Sivat paratavam nasti." "There is no being (God) superior to Siva." This seems to have been aimed particularly against the Ramanuja propagandists, perhaps because of a few prominent conversions. This challenge was openly thrown out, and naturally enough everybody pointed to Ramanuja as the person whose assent ought to be obtained. Ramanuja was summoned to appear in the royal presence.

Ramanuja's friends feared danger, and to avoid it Kurathalvar undertook to personate Ramanuja. Assuming the robes of the *sannyasi*, Kurathalvar went along with the venerable Periyanambi to the the Chola Court, while Ramanuja assuming the dress of a house-holder and at the head of a small body of adherents betook himself to the kingdom of the Hoysala Bitti Deva. Travelling along the banks of the Kaveri Ramanuja settled down at Saligram where he lived for a period of 12 years. While here Bitti Deva was just carving out for himself a kingdom along the southern marches of the Chalukya kingdom of Vikramaditya and the Chola frontier in the north-west.

CONVERSION OF BITTI DEVA.

A daughter of the king was possessed and after failing in all other attempts at exorcism Ramanuja's aid was called in. Sure enough the ghost was raised and Bitti Deva agreed to become the disciple of Ramanuja. This could not, however, be without overcoming the Jains in controversy, as the king is reputed to have been a Jain. Ramanuja had the best of it in the disputation and the bulk of the Jains either embraced the

Ramanuja *darsana* or were ordered to be ground down in oil mills. This latter threat, however, was not carried into effect through the intervention of Ramanuja. Ramanuja returned to Saligram.

DISCOVERY AND CONSECRATION OF THE MELLKOTE TEMPLE.

It was while here that Ramanuja's stock of *namam* (the white earth which serves for the Vaishnava caste mark on the forehead) ran out of stock and Ramanuja was much concerned. He dreamt overnight that there was a hill of that material, not far from Tondanur, where he made the acquaintance with Bitti Deva. Following the clue he obtained in his dream, and through the good offices of Vitala Deva (Bitti Deva) Ramanuja got the spot marked out is his dream dug up; when lo! there appeared beneath a small shrine. He then got is consecrated as Tirunarainapuram (Melukote of the maps). Thinking of a suitable image for this shrine, he dreamt of the image of Ramaprya which was at Delhi in possession of the daughter of the ruler at the time. He had to undertake a journey to Northern India again. Having got possession of the image somewhat miraculously, he returned with it. As the princess proved inconsolable without her pet image, the (king whoever he was) sent a party of men to bring back Ramanuja, who found shelter in a Panchama village. It is out of gratitude for this protection that he ordained the admission of the latter into the temple on the car festival. The consecration of the image and the completion of the temple are placed in 1021 Saka or 1099 A.D., which appears to antidate the event much. He had to make good his position here again as against everybody else, and held a successful disputation against the Bauddhas of Padmagiri (Sravana Belgola). He then resided at Tirunarainapuram expecting news from the South.

RAMANUJA RETURNS TO SRIRANGAM.

While Ramanuja was busy doing the important things detailed above, Kurathalvar and Periyanambi went to the Chola court in obedience to the royal summons. There the question was put to them whether they subscribed to the statement *Sivat Parataram Nasti!* Kurathalvar subscribed with a reservation *Dronamasti Tatahaparam.* "There is Drona above Siva"! taking Siva in the sense of a measure, Drona being a bigger measure. For this impertinence the angry king ordered the putting out of the eyes of the two Vaishnavas. Periyanambi, a venerable old man, died on the way; but the sturdier Kurathalvar, nothing daunted, returned and lived at Srirangam. After a time the Chola ruler died of a carbuncle, which the Vaishnavas put down to be the result of the ruler's cruelty to the devoted adherents of Ramanuja. News of the death of the Chola was taken to Ramanuja by the messenger whom he had sent to condole with Kurathalvar in his misfortune. On receipt of this somewhat assuring news, Ramanuja made up his mind to return.

ORGANISATION OF THE ADHYAYANOTSAVA AND THE COLLECTION OF THE PRABANDHA.

Consoling his beneficent disciple as best he could,

Ramanuja had to set about arranging matters for the *Adhyayanotsava* (an annual festival for the recitation of the works of the Tamil Saints) for which it was the practice to fetch the image of Nammalvar from Alvar Tirunagari in the Tinnevelly District. This having been a year of heavy rainfall it was found impossible to bring the image of the Alvar all the way. Ramanuja in consequence consecrated a shrine and restored the image of the Alvar in Srirangam itself, so that no similar difficulty might be experienced for the future. It was on the occasion of this festive celebration that one of the disciples of Kurathalvar dedicated the centum in honour of Ramanuja on the model of the decad of Madhurakavi on Nammalvar. Amudan of Arangam the author of the centum, it would appear, was the Smartha manager of the temple at Sirangam, and had been not over accommodating to the Vaishnava apostle or his disciples. When his old mother was drawing near her end, the son dutifully enquired if she desired anything he might do for her. She wished that either Ramanuja himself or one of his nominees might be invited to accept food of him on the occasion of her funeral ceremonies. Amudan had no alternative but to make the request of Ramanuja, who advised that his indomitable disciple Kurathalvar might be asked. The latter accepted the invitation and demanded for satisfaction the keys of the temple which Amudan surrendered and became hence-forward the disciple of Kurathalvar. This Amudan in his new-born zeal composed the centum and begged hard that it might be accepted. Ramanuja accepted the dedication and permitted its inclusion in the prabandha 4000 at the earnest pleadings of his first disciples. Having made provision for the regular annual recital of this 4000, Ramanuja got images of the Alvars and Andal set up in Srirangam and other important places, where also similar annual celebrations were ordained.

CONSECRATION OF THE GOVINDARAJA SHRINE AT TIRUPATHI.

He then paid a visit to Alvar Tirunagari and on his return heard that his maternal uncle at Tirupathi was no more. He then repaired thither and got the funeral ceremonies duly performed by the elder of the two cousins of his, the younger of whom he had long regarded as his son in apostolic succession. It was while he was yet here that he heard that the Govindaraja temple at Tirupathi had been overthrown and the image cast into the sea. He caused the image to be brought over, and housed it in the temple at the foot of the sacred hill where again he caused to be set up the images of the Alvars and Andal as elsewhere.

PILGRIMAGE TO HOLY PLACES.

He then returned to Srirangam by way of Kanchi and Madhurantakam. He then went to Tirumalirunjolai and Srivilliputtur to complete his round of pilgrimage to the sacred shrines of Vishnu in the South. Having thus established his influence throughout South India and having organised and popularised the teachings of Visishtadvaita-Vedanta he could now think his mission was at an end.

ARRANGEMENT OF THE SUCCESSION.

He arranged for the continuance of his teaching by nominating seventy-four among the worthiest of his followers. Of this number four had special custody of the Bhashya, one among whom had the Prabhanda teaching also. This one was no other than his cousin son Pillan, who became the actual successor of Ramanuja.

While he was preparing to depart this world he found the most indomitable among his companions anticipate him in this as well. Having got his funeral rites duly performed, Ramanuja felt himself quite at the end of his mission when again at the importunate entreaty of his disciples, he had to permit 3 of his own representations consecrated and set up in Srirangam, Sriperumbuthur and Tirunarainapuram. This example had been followed later on and every Vishnu temple in the South has, as a necessary adjunct, a little shrine for Ramanuja. Consoling his sorrowing disciples and companions, Ramanuja felt the call and passed away quietly having completed his 120th year in this world.

The above, in brief, is an outline of the life of Ramanuja, as the most authoritative tradition has it. This tradition has an inevitable tendency to gather volume, as time passes, and there have been as many varieties of this biography as are found interested hagiologists. But this account relies particularly on two contemporary works which have special claims for our acceptance. Neither of them is a professed biography and both of them were written for the acceptance-of contemporaries and one of them had been read before Ramanuja and obtained his imprimatur. This is the work of Amudan of Arangam and consists of one hundred stanzas in Tamil included in the Prabandha of the Tamil part of the Vaishnava lore. The other is the work of a disciple also, by name Vaduhanambi, (or in Sanskrit Andhrapurana) perhaps because he was a Telugu man. This is called Yathiraja Vaibhavam and consists of 114 slokas. This work describes all that Ramanuja did in a way so free from exaggeration that it would strike one as being particularly reliable. The name of the author occurs among the 74 successors of first degree of Ramanuja and his obligation to the master is indicated in the sloka quoted hereunder.'

"Kamschid Kasminschid arthe prathiniyathathaya sanniyojyantharangair, thathra kshirartha kritye pratiniyathamaho dasamapyathyanarham Kurvan sriman yathisassvapathavinatha thathdasanudasam mamapyathyanthabaktam svahithamiva sadha gopayan sopi payat." Having ordered his most trusted disciples to accept particular offices, Ramanuja "who protected his worthy servant, servant of his servants, entrusted with the service of providing milk, may he prosper." It now remains to examine historically what truth there is in the above account from available historical material and how far certain impressions that prevail regarding Ramanuja and his teachings find justification from his life and times.

Having recounted the incidents in the life of Ramanuja in the previous sections of the paper, we shall now proceed to examine critically whether the main incidents of his life are what his disciples claim them to have been and whether recent research, so far as it bears upon these, lends any support to these as a whole. The following incidents will be examined seriatim, as they appear to be arranged in chronological order:—

1. Ramanuja's conversion of Yadavaprakasa, his preceptor.

2. His conversion of Yegnamurti, an Advaita Sannyasin.

3. Settlement of the Smartha Vaishnava dispute about the God at Tirupathi.

4. The Chola persecution of Ramanuja.

5. The Hoysala Vishnuvardhana's conversion.

6. Foundation of the temple at Tirunarayanapuram (Melukote).

7. The conversion of Amudan of Arangam, the author of Ramanuja Nurrandhadhi.

8. The consecration of the Govinda temple at the foot of the Tirupathi Hill.

For the purposes of this again we shall, as far as possible, have recourse to such works of reliable authority, as those of Ramanuja's contemporaries and immediate successors only.

i. Yadavaprakasa was an advaitic teacher of reputation at Conjeevaram. He was also a writer of authority in his philosophy; and in his days and after he was a leader of a school of thought, that as the best representative of advaitic exposition, Vedantha Desika quotes him and disputes his position. He is the reputed author of Yatidharma Samuchayam and of the Yadava Nikandu: according to others the two works are from separate persons. At any rate the Yadava of the former work is in all probability, the philosophical expounder of the advaitic system. In the face of these facts, it would appear impossible that he should have been the first convert to the teachings of his ex-disciple Ramanuja, whom he did not love overmuch as a disciple. So it does, and I had long thought that the story was a pious fabrication. There is no reference in the Yatidharma Samuchchayam to his conversion at all. This is a work which undertakes to examine what the duties of a sannyasi are according to the best authority; and he seems to hold that there is good authority for both classes of sannyasins—those with the sacred thread and tuft of hair on the head (the Vaishnava) and those without these adjuncts (the Saiva). Except a reference to the 'Prabhandas' in the invocatory verse and the invocation itself being addressed to Vishnu as Dattatrya, the work is non-committing in this particular. But the work, Ramanuja Nurrandhadbi of Amudan of Arangam, one of his own converts, refers often to success in disputation against great controversialists, but does not mention names though the references are such as would warrant the inference that they were in particular Yadavaprakasa and the sannyasin Yegnamurti (Stanzas 58, 64 and 88). But in two works of Vedanta Desika coming just three generations after or say about a century, we have direct references to the purpose. The first half of verse 13 of Ethiraja Saptati refers to "Svabhalat Uddhrita Yadavaprakasa" (he that had up-rooted with his own strength Yadavaprakasa). This need not necessarily mean conversion but that such was actually the case is clearly stated in one of his other works, Satadhushani.* *Vedanta Desika* followed *Ramanuja* at an interval of three generations only and we might take him as a sufficient authority for the fact, as he takes Yadava's opinions and seriously controverts them in other parts of his works.

ii. As to Yegnamurti's conversion we are not in a position to say anything as nothing more is known of him than the fact, perhaps of his having been a sannyasin (Ekadhandi).

iii. The question about Tirupathi is of far greater importance, the more so as there has recently been going on a lively controversy about the same subject

* I am obliged for this reference to Tarkathirtha Punditaratnam Kasturirangachar of Mysore.

असमीक्षितदशापरित्यक्तत्रयसूत्रैश्च यादवप्रकाशैः समीक्ष्यसंजातानुशयैः स्वेषप्रमाणमनुयुक्ता वासुदेवयात्रात्सवसमागत। ननादिगन्तवास्तव्यशिष्टाश्च प्रायश्चित्तमेव उत्तरंददुः भ्रष्टस्तर्हि असावितिचेन्न। प्रायश्चित्तात्पूर्वमेव तथात्वस्य प्राचीनैर्निश्चितत्वात्। तत्समुच्चितस्यैव मतिधर्मस्याद्यापि मानवादिवदविनागात् :—।

शतदूषणी—यतिलिङ्गभेदभङ्गम् 64

ततश्च परित्यक्तयज्ञोपवीतादिकेषु एकदण्डिकेष्वपि-अद्यापि आयुष्मती विप्रतिपत्तिः भास्करयादवप्रकाशादि ग्रन्थरसायन सेवयानिवर्तते ॥

शतदूषणी—अत्लेपकभमतङ्गम् 65

in the columns of the journals and papers consequent on Mr. Venkyya's reference to the temple having been Saivite in his official report. It will be seen that the Vaishnava account has it that the God on the hill had just lent his characteristic weapons, the disc and the conch, to the Tondaman Chakravarti. Let it be noted here, in passing, that this evidently refers to the conquest of Kalingam by Karunakara Tondaman about 1111 A.D. Messrs. M. Narayanasami Iyer, B.A., B.L., and T. A. Gopinatha Rao, M.A., have both written concerning this in the *Sen Tamil.* The former inclines to the Vaishnava view and the latter to the Saiva. The question, therefore, needs to be examined with care. The following facts concerning the point appear to be agreed upon. The Tevaram hymners have not at all celebrated the shrine; the Vaishnava Alvars have. The Tamil epic Silappadhikaram has explicitly given the temple a Vaishnava character and there is no possibility of mistake here. On this account, therefore, Mr. Gopinatha Rao would bring the Silappadhikaram after Poygai Alvar (whether he brings it also after Ramanuja is not quite clear, though he shows a leaning to bring it to the middle of the 12th century). This gentleman holds that the original God was Subrahmaniya as the place is called 'Ilangoil' and the God is referred to once or twice as 'Kumara' though not without other adjuncts. The latter is quite decisive according to him. So it would be, if the premises have been quite as they are represented to be. One fundamental defect here is the taking out of words without reference to their context. Mr. Gopinath Rao refers to the God being known as Balajee among the Northerners. This may be, but Balajee is not exclusively applied to Subrahmaniya, if applied to him at all. I have here numbers of persons known as Balajee, but the word stands for Balakrishna. This is equally sound; there is something more. The early Alvars, Poyga Alvar, Bhutattar, Pey Alvar delight in referring to God in one of his aspects as a child either as Rama or Krishna preferably the latter. One has only to look through the writings of these to be convinced of this. Why they do so is beside the point. It is this Balakrishna—he is not so named in the work—that has given rise to the name Balajee.* Since, Krishna, as Vitoba is very popular in the Mahratta country. Anyhow this interpretation of Balajee is in keeping with the writings of the Alvars who had bestowed their best thoughts upon God's manifestation at Tirupathi. Pey Alvar lends the greatest support to this contention as to the nature of the deity. He refers to the God as இளங்குமரன் றன் விண்ணகர் (61); விளங்கனிக்குக் கன்றெறிந்தோன் வெற்பு (68); இளங்குமரர் கோமானிடம் (72) நான் முகத்தோன் நன்குறங்கில், வாய்ந்தகுழவியாய் (77). It will thus be seen that he refers to the same deity in the four different ways as above. They are of course to be taken synonymously. References one and three may be

---

* When last at Tirupathi I heard another version. When the Northerners first appeared at the shrine they were struck with the softly beautiful look of the image and exclaimed Bala (damsel). Hence the name Balajee as they say.

doubtful, but the other two must be sought to help us in the interpretation. Reference 2 clearly indicates one of the acts of young Krishna, and reference, 4, though not equally clearly, to an achievement of Vishnu, when Brahma was about to grant the boons sought of him by Ravana. If a more direct indication be needed, the stanza 62 makes it clear to any unprejudiced mind. There are a number of places sacred to Vishnu and the names given are Vaishnavite names *e.g.*, Tiruvarangam and Thirukudandhai—(Kumbhakonam). There is thus nothing to bear out the contention that the God there was ever meant to be Subrahmaniya. Stanza 63 of the same 3rd Tiruvandadi states clearly that the manifestation of God there is in the united form of Siva and Vishnu. This is borne out by the stanzas 5 & 98 of the 1st Tiruvandadi. This would, therefore, make it clear that the God was of the Harihara type. Then the question arises why it is that Ilango speaks of it as a Vishnu temple in such clear terms. The explanation perhaps would be that the temple had been known only as a Vishnu temple, though there was the duplex character in the idol. This could be noticed only by a devotee who was in close touch with the temple which Ilango could not pretend to have been. There would be nothing very strange about this if most people now-a-days do not know it. Its established reputation as a Vishnu temple accounts for the omission of Tirupathi by the Nayanmars of the Saivites. How then was it that the Saivites laid claim to it in the days of Ramanuja ? Ramanuja's time was remarkable for the revival of the Prabandam which was being taught much more widely than before. Besides this, Ramanuja's cousin's conversion must have made the Saivites alive to the danger of this Vaishnava neighbourhood. So on the old grounds of the dual form of the God they revived their claims, particularly as the ruling sovereign was likely to lean to the Saiva side. Naturally enough Ramanuja appealed to a trial by ordeal of some sort. Ever after, there appears to have been no dispute as to the character of the deity. This must have taken place sometime after 1111 A. D., the probable date of the conquest of Kalingam.

iv. The next item of importance in the life of Ramanuja is the Chola persecution. The Chola ruler at the time was Kulothunga, the Chalukya Chola (1070—1118 A. D.) The Cholas were Saivas most of them, but they were tolerant enough of other religions as well, while some of them even went the length of endowing Vishnu temples. This Kulothunga does not appear to have been particularly narrow-minded, as he made a grant even to the Bauddha settlement at Negapatam. But as the Vaishnava account itself has it, he was persuaded by others into compelling all to assent to the doctrine of the supremacy of Siva. This is not at all improbable considering that this was the period of great Saiva activity and the ruler was the special patron of Sekkilar. The general body of Vaishnavas do not appear to have been ill-treated, but Ramanuja's active work at Srirangam attracted attention and ended in the blinding of Kurathalvar and the old preceptor of Ramanuja himself. This must have taken place about the nineties of the 11th century. And Ramanuja was compelled to leave the country. His immigration into the Mysore country brings us to the next important incident in his life.

v & vi. He moved up the Kavery and settled at Saligram, wherefrom he had been invited to the head-quarters of Vitala Deva Raya or Bitti Deva. This latter could not have been the ruling sovereign at the time as his brother was alive to the end of the century and a few years later. During the last years of the century he was still active in the Gangavadi frontier, and it was while here that he must have met Ramanuja. His elder brother "had for his God Isa" and this meant perhaps he was a Saiva. Bitti Deva was converted and he helped Ramanuja in the restoration of the temple of Narayana at Melukote. I have elsewhere* shown that the persecution of the Jains ascribed to Vishnuvardhana is hardly supported by facts. The consecration of the temple at Melukote is placed in the year 1099 A. D. twelve years after Ramanuja's arrival at Saligram. This might have been the case as Ramanuja would have taken care not to provoke the hostility of the ruler of his new domicile. Vishnuvardhana thenceforward supported the cause of Ramanuja and encouraged Vishnavaism. He went on building temples and endowing them, not without supporting the other temples and creeds as well, though not perhaps to the same extent. This activity culminated

* *Mysore Review* for March, 1905. (Vide Appendix.)

in the building and consecration of the temple at Belur in (or about) 1117 A.D.* There is nothing improbable in the date, as it was in this year that he could claim to have become master of the Gangavadi. So Ramanuja must have lived in Mysore for nearly a quarter of a century. It was the death of the Chola Kulothunga in 1118 A. D. that enabled him to return. But then there is perhaps an inconsistency with respect to dates. As the Guruparamparai has it, it would appear that the Chola died soon after the blinding of the two friends of Ramanuja; but in actual fact, if the date 1099 A. D. be taken as correct for the Melukote incident, which appears too early to be true, the death of the persecuting Chola came many years after. This kind of accuracy, it would be too much to expect in an account such as we have and of its professed character.

vii. The next incident of importance is the conversion of Amudan of Arangam, the manager of the temple at Srirangam, a non-Vaishnava. For this we have evidence of the convert himself. He is the author of the Ramanuja Nurrandhadhi and in verses 3, 4 & 7 of the work he makes it clear that he was a convert by favour of Ramanuja and Kurathalvar. In verses 8, 21, he clearly describes Ramanuja's relation to the Alwars and Nadhamuni and Alavandar (Yamunaithuraivar), in spite of opinions to the contrary by scholars who implicitly believe in the opinion of Dr. Caldwell. Not only this. The centum (in fact 108) of his verses gives in a small span, mostly allusively but

---

Hassan vol of the Epigraphia Carnataka Ins. Belur 58 & 71.

clearly enough, the main achievements of Ramanuja and thus becomes the contemporary authority for mos of the facts of Ramanuja's life as detailed above. The moderation of tone and sobriety of language commend its authority the more, as else Ramanuja would not have been persuaded into including it among the Pranandam 4000.

viii. Lastly comes the construction and consecration of the Govinda shrine at the foot of the Tirupathi Hill. This affords the best clue to the date of Ramanuja. The Guruparamparai gives this as the last act of a busy life under circumstances which, thanks to the researches of Brahma Sri R. Raghava Iyengar, Court Pandit of Ramnad and Editor of the *Sen Tamil*, the organ of the Madura Tamil Sangam, prove to be quite historical. The story it will be remembered is that the Govinda Raja temple at Chidambaram having been removed from the premises of the great Siva temple, Ramanuja and his disciples got the idol enshrined in a new temple at Tirupathi. In a number of historical works relating to the period, particularly in the Kulothunga Cholan Ula of Ottakuthan,* this achievement is ascribed to Kulothunga II, the son and successor of Vikrama Chola and one of the patrons of Kuthan himself. There it is described that he renovated the Saiva temple and plated the roofing with gold—incidentally mentioning that the " God Vishnu had been sent back to his original shrine—the sea." †

---

* Sen Tamil Vol. III, Pt. 5 pp. (166—167).

† Sen Tamil Vol. III, Pt. 8 pp. (301—302.)

This would mean not only the removal but the throwing of the image into the sea. In another, there is a reference to Kulothunga's having rooted out the minor Gods from the great shrine. This must have taken place in the reign of Kulothunga II (cir. 1123-1146). That the Vaishnavas were enabled to enshrine the God at Tirupathi perhaps shews the limitation of the Chola authority at the time or their indifference to the fact, provided the obnoxious God had been removed from the hallowed presence of their "Holy of Holies," a place full of the most narrow-minded of the Saivites. That the Vishnu shrine was previously in the temple at Chidambaram is borne out by a reference in the works of Manikka Vasagar (Tiruchchirambalakkovai, 86). There is absolutely no reason to doubt the authority of these works about this particular and this would give us the ultimate limits of Ramanuja's active life. According to the traditional account Ramanuja lived for 120 years from 1017 A.D.—1137 A.D. Some object to this length and regard it as a fabrication just to give the reformer the 'Mahadasa' as it is called. It is a matter of very small consequence to us whether he lived the 120 years or no. What is more important for our purposes is that his was a long and active life and covered three reigns of the Cholas :—Kulothunga I (1070 A.D. to 1118 A.D.), Vikramachola (1118 A.D.—1135 A.D.), Kulothunga II. (1123—1146 A.D.) Ramanuja's active life might, therefore, be safely referred to the last quarter of the 11th and the first-half of the 12th century A.D.

Sri Ramanujacharya

HIS PHILOSOPHY.

BY

MR. T. RAJAGOPALACHARYAR, M.A., B.L.

THE TERM 'VISISHTADWAITA' EXPLAINED.

THE Visishtadwaita is so-called because it inculcates the *adwaita* or oneness of God, with *visêsha* or attributes. It is, therefore, 'qualified non-dualism.' God alone exists; all else that is seen is His manifestation, attribute, or *Sakti*. Such attributes are *chit* or the individual souls and *achit* or matter. The adwaitic position is also that God alone exists and all else is manifestation. Herein is the common element between the two views; but the Adwaitin regards the manifestation as unreal and temporary, and as a result of *Avidya* or Nescience. In consequence, the one Brahman is without any attribute, in his view. Ramanuja and his school regard the attributes as real, and permanent, but subject to the control of the one Brahman in all their modifications and evolutions. The oneness of God is compatible with the existence of attributes, as the latter are incapable of existing alone, and so do not constitute independent things. They are called the *prakaras* or the modes, *sesha* or the accessories, and *niyamya* or the controlled, of the one Brahman. The word Brahman is thus used either to denote the central unity, when it becomes possible to speak of the souls and matter, as its attributes, or to denote the combined trinity when the whole universe may properly be described as consisting of Brahman and Brahman alone. The Visihtadwaitin does not make the unphilosophical statement that the souls are absolutely independent entities, endowed with the capacity of separate existence and activity, apart from Brahman.

THE FUNDAMENTAL ATTRIBUTES.

The Brahman (we use the word in the first of the above senses) is Intelligence. It is something more— it is the Knower. Where attributes are denied, and all that exists is homogenous intelligence, as in the Adwaita, there can be no knower; for there is nothing to know. But for the Visishtadwaitin, Brahman is a knower, and the variety, philosophically essential for knowledge, is furnished by the attributes. Brahman is Bliss, *i.e.*, he is blissful; for a mixture of the opposite, pain, is unimaginable in his case. It will thus be seen that besides the attributes of souls and matter, which may be called 'the concrete attributes' if such a phrase may be used, Brahman has various abstract attributes qualities strictly so called, denoting his perfection from various points of view. The Visishtadwaitin considers 'Intelligence' as partaking of the dual character of an abstract and a concrete attribute; and he instances 'light' as an example of the possibility of such an attribute. Intelligence is the essence of Brahman; it is an attribute as well, in its nature of universal pervasion. Again Brahman is real, *satya*. By this is understood that he is without *vikara* or modification of any kind. The souls and matter are *asatya* or unreal, which again means that they are subject to modification, which is necessarily an element of impurity. In the case of souls, this modification takes the form of expansion or contraction of Intelligence. In mineral, plant or animal life, the soul, under *karmic* control, is dull or of suppressed Intelligence. The modifications of matter are of a more serious kind. In the creation and expansion of the universe, matter undergoes a real modification of its nature. Such change is called *parinama* or evolution, as contrasted with *vivarta* or apparent variation, which is the view of the Adwaitin. The Visishtadwaitin holds that, in spite of the souls and matter being pervaded by Brahman, any modifications of them though under Brahman's control, do not touch His essence; just as the Adwaitin maintains that the operation of *Avidya* do not affect the one Reality. The 'unreality' of the cosmos is thus another point of agreement between the Adwaitin and the Visihtadwaitin; but this, it must be admitted, is merely a nominal agreement, considering the important diversity in their conceptions of the unreality. The Visishtadwaitin would thus call Brahman, '*Sat*,' and the rest '*Asat*'; in a narrower sense; he reserves the epithet 'Asat' to Matter, which undergoes change in its essence, unlike the souls whose essence is like to the Brahman's and never changes.

TWO STATES OF BRAHMAN.

There are two states of existence for the Brahman. One is absolute quiescence or *pralaya*, when all the souls and matter exist in Him in deep sleep as it were. No differentiation is possible in that stage between the souls and matter; these are then, as it were, non-existent. '*Sat* alone exists, one without a second.' Existence is the only phrase that can be applied to the Brahman then, as volition, not to speak of creation, is potential or has not commenced to work. Then begins the second stage, creation. To the Adwaitin, creation is a negative, an unreal, act. It is the clouding of the pure Intelligence of Brahman by the inexplicable Avidya, which produces the manifestation of apparent diversity. The Visishtadwaitin considers creation as a positive volitional effort of the Brahman to display real diversity, by actualising the energy for change which is innate in both the souls and matter. *Sa Aikshata bahu syam prajayèya iti.* 'He thought, may I become many, may I grow forth.' The *antah pravesa* 'entry within' which the Upanishads speak of as taking place at creation is not strictly true. To the Visishadwaitin, it means only the Brahman's willing to develop His inseparable attributes, souls and matter; for Brahman was 'within' even before creation. To the Adwaitin, the *antah pravesa* is entirely metaphorical. The language of the *Parinàma Vada* is used in his view, merely for facility of comprehension.

THE PURPOSE OF CREATION.

The ethical justification for creation is Justice.

The fruits of actions (karma) have to be bestowed, equally and impartially, and Brahman does this by endowing souls with appropriate bodies of various kinds and giving room for further functioning and display of free-will within limits; the further evolution depends on the manner in which the individual uses his opportunities. As karma is, in the Hindu view, beginningless, it becomes unnecessary to account for its origin. To the objection that Brahman could have no purpose, being without wants, in engaging itself in creation, the reply is, in the words of the author of the Sutras, *lokavat tu lila kaivalyam* (II. 1·33). it is mere recreation. as in ordinary life. In other words, as no compulsion can be predicated of the Brahman to evolve the universe, the Visishtadwaitin accounts for it by the only other possible alternative, that it is mere recreation for the Brahman, but the strictest justice for the souls concerned. Sankara adds the explanation that His innate nature (*svabhava*) is to create, which does not carry us much further, and then reminds us that the whole discussion is unreal, as Brahman is never the agent of creation.

THE AUTHORITY OF REVELATION.

To the Visishtadwaitin, as to the Adwaitin, the Vedas and Smritis are the sole and independent authority for the knowledge of Brahman. Reason has no operation except in matters perceptible by the senses. Transcendental notions as those with respect to the nature and attributes of Brahman and the souls, can only be got from Revelation. This position appears illogical, dethroning, as it does, *Reason*, the accepted instrument of correct conclusion in all processes of thought. To explain this anomaly, we have to dwell a little on the exact place assigned to reason by Sankara as well as Ramanuja. Reason is an indefinite word. It depends for its correctness, on the intellectual capacity of the person arguing, the extent of his information and other circumstances. Until a fallacy is exposed, an argument is apparently sound. Then it is upset and the conclusion has to be reached by other reasonings. This want of finality in mere reason is referred to in the Sutras (II.1-11) and is the cause of the Vedantic systems rejecting it as a sufficient authority in the knowledge of Brahman as the Nyayikas did. The argument from design may at best establish a highly endowed intelligent first cause or causes, but could not lead to the conception of a perfect Brahman as first cause. And so, the help of mere reason as a sufficiently competent determining factor in the establishment of Brahman, as first cause, is rejected. This must not be taken to mean that the Hindu Vedantins reject argumentation in their philosophy. Every page of their writings is a standing monument of their skill in the subtlest reasonings. According to them the purpose of reasoning is two-fold. It has, in the first place, full scope in matters which do not transcend the senses. In the second place, it is a valuable adjunct in ontology, where the texts of the Vedas are to be construed. As it so happens that most important texts are liable to be disputed as to their meanings, it goes without saying that there is full room for logical interpretation with respect to them. To say that explicit Vedic texts are unquestionable authorities means one of two things, either that we take them as the conclusions of great minds reached after acute reasoning, on matters which our feeble intellects could not sufficiently comprehend or we consider them to be the records of unique direct experiences of men who had trained their powers of mental perception by methods to which we have no access. Neither position is inconceivable or necessarily absurd. So many scientific positions are accepted by the general body of educated men all over the world on the faith of representations that those positions have been verified by some one by actual experiments. There may be danger of mistakes and mis-statements in either case; but those like Sankara and Ramanuja, who do not feel the position of an agnostic satisfactory or comfortable, have preferred to base their ontological position on revelation, while fully trusting to their capacity for ratiocination to meet objections on the part of those who do not subscribe to the authority of the Vedas. Between these two, there is, however, a difference. Sankara includes the Srutis and Smritis among ephemeral things whose purpose is served when once oneness is realised. Ramanuja considers them as always authoritative and as expressive of the eternal commands of the Deity whose breath they are said to be. An important difference arises between these two thinkers, based on this distinction. In Sankara's view the compulsory nature of ordained duties last only till an individual has realised by thinking his unity with God. Ramanuja considers the performance of such duties obligatory as long as life and physical power endure. (See Sutras III. 4.32-35.)

There are also certain assertions in Ramanuja's religious tenets which must be unacceptable to those who do not believe in revelation or adopt his interpretation. Such are his eternally free souls (*nityas*), heaven conceived as a distinct place apart from and outside the changeable universe (though not outside Brahman), the existence of the Deity in physical forms of various kinds, the peculiar paths of souls on their release from the body, and so on. Belief in these is based on express texts and no reasoning can be called to prove them. It is Ramanuja's contention that reasoning is equally powerless to disapprove them. And a disapproval of these in no way affects Ramanuja's conclusions, as regards the nature of Brahman and its relation to souls and matter, as philosophical positions consonant to abstract reasoning.

MODE OF RECONCILIATION.

We now come to Ramanuja's mode of reconciling Vedic texts. Western scholars have tried to arrange chronologically the principal Upanishads and to discern, in some of them, partial truths; in others, crude statements; in others again, the completest insight into things transcendental that may be given to man. How far this discussion is convincing we shall not stop to examine. Where passages in the same Upanishads appear to conflict, as in the *Chandogya*, the *Brihad-*

Aranyaka, or the *Isa-Vasya*, it is evident that the ordinary rules of interpretation must be resorted to, to arrive at a consistent meaning. The respect which Hindus have entertained for the Upanishads on account of their antiquity has prevented them from considering any of them as of inferior authority to the rest. It follows that a consistent doctrine has to be attempted out of at least the principal Upanishads. This is what Sankara and Ramanuja have attempted to do, each in his own way. And this is indeed what Badarayana, the first interpreter of the Upanishads known to us, has himself done in the Sutras.

Professor Deussen and others have conjectured that Badarayana had a partiality for the Chandogya and hence the frequent reference to it in the topics discussed. Indian scholars thoroughly equipped with an intimate acquaintance with "the immense and highly technical philosophical literature, which is only just beginning to be studied and comprehended, in part, by European scholars," to use the words of Dr. Thibant, have ascertained that, in the two Mimamsas, the passage discussed in each adhikarana are only typical and not exhaustive and that the order of exposition is mainly based on logical sequence. It follows that there is no justification for the view that one or two Upanishads are specially intended as the repository of philosophical truths to the exclusion of other Upanishads.

The texts of the Upanishads referring to the Supreme Self are of two kinds. Some speak of Him as *nirguna*, attributeless. Others describe him as having attributes or qualities like wisdom, power, etc. As truth can be only one, the natural question arises whether these texts can be reconciled in any manner. Sankara's view is that predominance must be given to the *nirguna* texts, as the others have the effect of limiting the Infinite, which should not be done. Hence texts like '*Ekam eva Adwaitiyam*,' one only, without a second,' *neha nana Asti*,' there is here no diversity, etc. are interpreted by him, without much straining, as establishing the absolute oneness of the Brahman. And the other texts are relegated to an inferior position and made to refer to an imaginary and inferior Brahman called *apara* or *karya* Brahman, *i.e.*, the Brahman in conjunction with its creative power called *maya*. Ramanuja's difficulty seems to be that this sharp division of the passages into those referring to the higher and those referring to the lower Brahman is not easily and directly inferable from the texts themselves. On the other hand, the passages are so mixed up that it is impossible to say that this distinction, if true, was ever prominently kept up. His reconciliation is, therefore, as follows: the texts of the Upanishads do not inculcate an attributeless Brahman; the attributes are real and not the result of Avidya; the texts referring to those attributes expound the Brahman, as He is, with the souls and matter as His inseparable *modes*. Brahman is one, only in His compound nature, as described already. The texts denying any attributes for Him are to be taken as meaning that He has no low or inauspicious attributes, such as liability to changes, death, sorrow, etc. The texts as to creation, as mentioned already, mean a real modification of the attributes, souls and matter of the Brahman and do not mean that Brahman becomes suffused with Nescience and imagines a variety. The souls are many and God is immanent, both in them and in matter. The texts which speak of unity and deny variety do so of the totality of the Brahman with his attributes. Texts which deny a second to Brahman, mean that there is no other controlling power in the universe apart from Him. Texts which deny the possibility of knowing Brahman, do not mean that he cannot be the object of thought, as there is no thinker; they mean only that His wonderful and priceless excellences or qualities could not be adequately described. Else, according to Ramanuja, they would conflict with hosts of passages which prescribe knowledge of Brahman and ascribe qualities to Him. The text of the Brihad Aranyaka II. 3. 6. which contains the famous words "*neti neti*" "not so, not so" and is taken by Sankara to teach the negation of all attributes is interpreted by Ramanuja (Sutras. III. 2. 21) as merely denying the possibility of adequate knowledge of the Brahman. "This interpretation" says he, "is confirmed by the fact that after the negative phrase comes an epithet of Brahman as 'the True of the True, for the Pranas are the True'." Ramanuja interprets this text to mean that the Pranas or the individual souls are *satya* or 'true,' *i. e.*, not subject to change in their essence, while the Supreme Self is

4

altogether real or unchangeable. "He is, therefore, more eminently *true* than they (the souls) are."

THE THEORY OF CAUSATION.

The theory of causation has profoundly exercised the minds of all Hindu philosophers; the Vedantins, like the Sankhyas, maintain the oneness of cause and effect in essence, as opposed to the logicians who maintain that they are different. In what sense, then, is the world which is an effect, one with its cause? Badarayana has a topic discussing this point. (Sutras, I. IV. 23, etc.) Here he maintains that the Brahman is not merely the instrumental cause, but also the material cause of the universe. He is, in the position, not merely of the potter but also of the mud, to give an illustration familiar to Indian philosophers. A succeeding Sutra, (I. 4. 27,) refers to the way in which Brahman as the cause becomes the effect. It is by '*pari-nama*' or owing to modification. In Ramanuja's view the oneness of cause and effect arises from the fact that the cause is the Brahman in the *sukshma* or subtle state, when the souls and matter are undeveloped and the effect is Brahman also, now comprised of the Supreme Self and the souls and matter, the latter in a fully developed state.* Sankara, practically admitting the interpretation of the Sutras given above, would. however, explain the modification as '*Vivarta*' really, *i.e.*, phenomenal creation by Brahman as influenced by Avidya or Maya. That the

* The phrase Visishtadwaitam is sometimes explained as the oneness or identity and the two *Visishta* entities mentioned in the text, as cause and effect.

two philosophers are entirely at variance in their view of this oneness is also clear from their respective commentaries on the important Sutra II-1-15, (14, in Sankara's numbering) a discussion of which would be out of place in this brief exposition. We would only draw attention to an important and suggestive statement of Sankaracharya, at the close of his commentary of the above Sutra, that Badarayana, in his view, omits to contradict the reality of the manifested world and adopts the language of the *Parinama Vada*, for the purpose of facilitating the exposition of the saguna meditations later on in the work.

THE DOCTRINE OF NESCIENCE.

Ramanuja's Sribhashya is remarkable for the lengthy disquisition on various topics by which his actual commentary on the Sutras is preceded. In this disquisition, he treats of various controversial points and expounds fully his differences of views from those of Sankara. One of the most important of these is his statement of objections to the theory of Maya or Avidya, which is a fundamental one in Sankara's philosophy and is, at the same time, the most vulnerable point in it. Is this Avidya different from or identical with Brahman ? The former view would seem to undermine Sankara's doctrine of oneness and the latter is equally untenable. Sankara cuts the Gordian knot by boldly declaring that it (the Avidya) is *Sadasadanirvachaniya*, *i. e.*, it is indescribable as either existing or non-existing. Ramanuja expounds at great length his difficulties as to the tenability of the Maya theory, under seven heads, a clear account of which is to be found in Professor Ranghacharya's 'Analytical outline' prefixed to his valuable translation of the Sri Bhashya, Vol. I. Ramanuja's objections are of this wise: The Avidya cannot operate on the Brahman, directly, for His nature is Intelligence and this would repel Nescience by its intrinsic merit. Nor can it operate on the individual souls, for these are the outcome of the action of Avidya and cannot, therefore, be acted upon in anticipation. Again, to state that Nescience clouds the Brahman is impossible, for that would mean that Brahman's luminous nature is thereby destroyed, a position which is not admissible. Avidya, again, as defined by Sankara, is in Ramanuja's view, inconceivable, as the simultaneous possession of two opposite characters, as existence and non-existence, cannot be predicated of anything in human conception. Ramanuja, further, does not think that to describe Avidya as 'indescribable' really strengthens the position of Sankara; for if a thing is absolutely indescribable, it must be non-existent as an entity. Then Ramanuja points out that such an Avidya cannot be proved to exist by any known means of proof including Vedic or Smriti texts; if such an Avidya should exist, it is irremovable, says Ramanuja, for the knowledge of attributeless Brahman required to remove it, is according to him an impossible thing, such a Brahman not being provable. Lastly, such an Avidya is irremovable for another reason. In Ramanuja's view the ignorance, being the result of karma, can be removed only by enjoined action and meditation. Mere knowledge of Brahman cannot remove it. For all these reasons, Ramanuja concludes that the theory of Maya is untenable and opposed to the tenor of the Vedic texts.

CONCLUSION.

It is not the purpose of this sketch to explain all Ramanuja's objections to Sankaracharya's views. What has been attempted is only the setting forth of Ramanuja's views on important points with just so much reference to the doctrines of Sankara, as is necessary to understand Ramanuja. To really grasp the vital differences between these two eminent philosophers, and to arrive at a proper estimate of their relative merits, would mean a thorough discussion of three important questions, namely, (1) who is the better interpreter of the Upanishads, (2) who has more accurately represented the views of the Vedanta Sutras, and (3) who is entitled to greater respect as a philosophical thinker. These are questions of so difficult a nature that they are entirely beyond our scope and capacity. Enough has, however, been said to show that Ramanuja when he becomes better known, would most certainly be deemed entitled to a high place among the world's philosophers, and his system, though not possessing the simplicity or universality of Sankaracharya's, is yet an eminently sound one, compatible with the admission of the reality of the cosmos and a high conception of the nature and attributes of the Deity.

Ramanuja and Vaishnavism.*

BY

RAO BAHADUR PROF. M. RANGACHARYA, M.A.

VAISHNAVAISM is a very old form of religion known to the History of Civilisation in India. How old it is, it is not now possible to determine; but it is certain that its sources may be traced to the Vedas. Vishnu in Vedic literature is seen to be a solar deity, and is conceived as an all-pervading god. It is in accordance with a very widely accepted Indian derivation of the word to interpret Vishnu as a pervader; and the conception of this same god as Trivikrama—as the god who was able to cover the whole universe in three strides—is also distinctly Vedic in origin. Moreover, as a god he is said to have his place in the supreme heaven, in *Vishnoh paramam padam*, as it is called in the Vedas. Modern European scholars consider that this *parama-pada* of Vishnu is, in all probability, the position of the sun in the zenith. This is obviously the highest position conceivable that may be occupied by any object during the day. Thus Vishnu was of old a solar deity who occupied the highest heaven, and was at the same time capable of pervading with his light and life all the three worlds making up the visible universe, the earth-world, the mind-world and the sky-world. The all-pervading god and the god who occu-

*From a lecture by Rao Bahadur Prof. M. Rangachariar, M.A. of the Madras Presidency College.

pies the highest heaven—such evidently is the conception underlying Vishnu in Vedic literature. From this conception as its source has arisen Vaishnavaism, which, in its various forms, is now recognised to be the most predominant and the most popular religion among the Hindus. To ascertain and describe the position occupied by Ramanuja in relation to the progress and development of this great religion is the main aim which I intend to keep in view in my lecture.

The primary conception underlying the original deity is a matter of great importance in determining the course of development of the religion associated with that deity. This can be amply illustrated by means of instances that may be gathered from the history of religions. There is, for instance, another solar deity in Vedic literature, who goes by the name of MITRA; and this god Mitra, understood as the Sanskrit language requires, is the sun-god conceived as a friend. This Mitra is not merely a god of our Vedas, but is a god known to the Zend-Avesta of the Parsees as well. He seems therefore to have been a god held in honor by the Iranian as well as by the Indian Aryas even before they separated from each other. That separation must of course have taken place very very long ago. It may well be that this Mitra was a deity worshipped in Persia before Zoroaster taught his religion—the modern religion of the Parsees. A great French savant, Ernest Renan, has solemnly remarked that, if Christianity had not gone to Europe, in all probability Mitraism would have become the religion of

Europeans. In saying this he evidently pays a very high compliment to this religion of MITRA and draws our attention to the tendency of that religion to be helpful to man in the way of encouraging in him purity love, piety and righteousness. He even seems to grant that the moral influence of that religion could indeed have been in no way inferior to that which Christianity has had among Europeans and Americans. Now, can it be said that the original conception of this god as a friend has had no power or part in determining the really superior moral merit of Mitraism? Surely its friendly god must have done a great deal in determining the line of development of that religion.

So it must have been in connection with the religion of Vishnu also. Moreover, we find here that, in very early times, another idea more prominently brought to light in connection with another Vedic deity, Bhaga, came to be associated with the religion of Vishnu. That other idea is in fact the conception of god Bhaga as a bestower of auspicious blessings. This god Bhaga is perhaps an older god than even Mitra. God Bhaga appears to have had an Indo-European history. He was known to the ancient religion of the Slavonians, to the ancient religion of the Parsees, and also to the ancient religion of the Aryas of this country. As the bestower of auspicious blessings, Bhaga seems to have been very highly honoured and held in great reverence as a typical god. This word *bhaga* in later Sanskrit literature came to assume many meanings. It may now mean the sun, but very frequently means good blessings and auspicious qualities and great powers. Thus the name of the sun-god, looked upon as a bestower of blessings and of auspicious powers, may easily be seen to have undergone a deterioration in meaning, so as to import not the god but the physical object symbolising the god, or those blessings and those powers whereof the god was originally conceived to be the bestower. When in this manner the earlier meanings of this word as the name of a god became almost forgotten among the people, the other later meaning naturally gained ground. It must be in consequence of an indentification of the god himself with the power of goodness that he possessed, that the word *bhaga* ceased to be the name of the god and came to denote chiefly his power of goodness and grace. After this took place, we observe a change in the structure of the name of the god: that name is no longer Bhaga but Bhagavat. This changed word means the possessor of those beneficent qualities and auspicious powers which have come to be represented by the word *bhaga*. In that way there arose a religion in which the worship of the Bhagavat was the chief element; and in it the Bhagavat came to be looked upon as the Supreme God. The religion which has been based on this worship of the Bhagavat is called the Bhagavata religion. It appears to be distinctly described in the *Mahabharata*. And even European and American critics seem to be fairly in agreement in holding that the *Mahabarata*, in its present form, must have been well known in

India not later than the 4th century before the Christian era. The *Mahabharata* is rightly conceived to be a work that could not have been produced at any one time by any one man. Although in the epic itself its authorship is ascribed to Vyasa, there is ample indication in it of frequent additions having been made to it in later times: and this sort of growth in size must have gone on with it for some centuries. If it is true that this growth reached its culmination about the 4th century before Christ, and if we have distinct references to the Bhagavata religion in the *Mahabharata*, then the worship of the Bhagavat must have been current for a fairly long time before that in India. That the Bhagavat may well be traced to the Vedic Bhaga is a point which does not seem to me to be in any manner improbable. There is some reason to believe that Sri-Krishna was probably the originator of the Bhagavata religion; and Megasthenes is considered to have been well aware of the prevalence of Krishna-worship in his days in North India. Now, if Vishnu and the Bhagavat are to be identified, as they seem to have been identified from very early times in this country, thereby Vaishnavism is naturally bound to become more comprehensive and to acquire a more expanded and more lovable moral meaning. Accordingly Vaishnavism came to mean in due time the worship of an all-pervading God, who is in the highest heaven, and is at the same time the bestower of all auspicious powers and benevolent blessings. Here, in this combined conception of God, we have the very heart, so to say, of Vaishnavism. From this central idea arose all the later developments of this religion, as also all its later adaptations to the needs of progressive Hindu life.

In the same manner as Vaishnavism, Saivasm also may be traced to the Vedas—to the Deity Rudra so well-known in Vedic literature. Vishnu is a solar Deity in the Vedas, as I mentioned to you already. Rudra is therein conceived to be Agni—the fire-god. From the Vedic conception of Rudra as the god of fire arose Saivism, even as from the conception of the sun-god arose the later worship of Vishnu as the one Supreme God. Why did these later developments and modifications in religion come into existence in this country, one may very well ask. Why was there the gradual overthrow of the old Vedic religion of sacrifices, and why the introduction of the later religions based on the *Upanishads*, the *Itihasas*, *Puranas* and *Agamas*? That is indeed an interesting question to ask. The development of thought in Indian civilisation made it necessary that the old Vedic religion of ritualism should be superseded by another religion, which had more of real life in it, and was more capable of satisfying the religious needs and aspirations of the human heart, irrespective of all considerations of race, caste and social status. Nevertheless, this new religion could not be altogether new. In fact the progress of religion is so effected in the history of all civilizations that no new religion can be absolutely or unmixedly new. When a new institution or a new idea has to be introduced among a people for their immediate benefit, it invariably happens that this new institution or new idea becomes implanted upon something that is really old. And the new idea or the new institution, growing in the midst of old surroundings, absorbs and assimilates a great deal of what is old from its environment: and in the result, the old and the new together sprout up in a new form so as to make the new product, viewed as a whole, more comprehensive, more beautiful and more helpful to the advancement of culture and character and civilization among the people. That is the way of progress everywhere. Whether we trace the origin, for instauce, of Buddhism or Christianity, or trace the course of civilization in China or Japan or France or England or India, we invariably find that new ideas and institutions grow in the midst of old environments and under the impulse of old forces which are still alive and actively in operation. We thus learn to see that every new growth is largely the result of the assimilation of much that is old with something that is new.

In the course of the development of the sacrificial religion of the Vedas, the influence of the priests at one time became so markedly preponderant that the gods themselves almost began to disappear from the vision of the sacrificers. And what loomed largely before their eyes was the performance of the sacrifice in accordance with the strict letter of the law. Another thing which also must have loomed largely was the rewarding of the sacrificial priests by the payment of valuable *dakshina* or honorarium to them. To what extent such a decline of the true religious spirit took place may be made out from the fact that some of the later *Mimamsakas*, when dealing with the question of who the *Devatas* are, to whom sacrifices are offered, hastily dismissed the question itself by giving out that we need not at all trouble ourselves about who the *Devatas* are. They went quite so far as to say that the *Dèvata* is simply that thing the name whereof is seen inflected in the dative case in sacrificial formulas like *Indraya svaha* for instance. "Who is Indra?" is the question asked, let us suppose. The reply is—Don't ask who he is. He may be anything or nothing. He is simply that thing the name of which is here in this formula inflected in the dative case." When such an answer is given to such a question, we may at once make out what relative importance must have been attached to the question of who or what the gods are, as compared with the numerous and complex details of the sacrificial ceremonial. When mere sacrificial details become too much all-absorbing, all considerations regarding who or what the deity is, what its powers are, why we should worship it, were thrown into the back-ground. In fact these and other more interesting details bearing upon the question of godhood rapidly went behind the curtain. As all thought bearing upon the vital question of godhood in religion disappeared in that manner, what happened to be left behind was nothing more than mere form overloaded with numerous complicated and unattractive details involving much useless expenditure of time, wealth and labour.

Naturally the common human heart would be prone to rebel against such a religion. There can indeed be no real life of any kind in an over-encrusted and fossilised shell of religion. There is nothing in it to touch the heart, and make it burn with the magic fire of spiritual fervour and moral emotion and sympathetic exaltation. It is too dry and too mechanical, too much of a sham to satisfy the deep religious longings of the aspiring and uplifted heart. In the early stages of its development Vedic religion was not like this either in its aim or in its practical use. From the very beginning it was indeed an earnest endeavour to rise from nature to Nature's God. In the hymns and prayers and chants addressed to the numerous nature-gods of the Vedas, a careful student may easily observe a growing tendency towards the realisation of what is sometimes called personal monotheism. The many gods of an earlier age become merged in the one God and are identified with Him: and this one God does not lose His divinity or His personality. Many consider that such a really divine and personal God has to be an essential element in all truly satisfying religions. Anyhow there must be for the common man in his religion something to grasp and to worship as a Supreme Power and Personality, who would lovingly come to help him in times of difficulties, and to whom he might with complete confidence surrender himself in all conditions of trial and sorrow and suffering. Religion has even been defined as a kind of self-surrender, as the surrender of themselves which men make to a Higher Power, feeling unable to look after themselves in this world of troubles and turmoils—in this world, wherein even the most thoughtful man feels that he is blindfolded and tossed about without any aid from any really capable and truly knowing guide. Such a puzzling thing is indeed this world of ours! It is in fact so full of mystery and so full of pitfalls to the earnest and thoughtful man that he naturally feels that it would be good for him to seek and obtain the support of a Supreme Power, so that he may throw himself entirely on the mercy of that Power and derive unerring guidance from It, and take safe refuge with It, whenever necessary. It is very proper that this kind of feeling should come to the human mind most commonly and most readily, particularly in times of great danger and difficulty. When such a trying hour comes, how will the over-formal sacrifice, with all its elaborate details of ritual, help the aching heart of the man in trouble? How will the idea that the deity may be nothing other than what happens to be represented by the word, which is inflected in the dative case in a sacrificial formula, help him? You can all easily see that a conception of the diety, such as this, will give him no help, no support, no comfort. It is therefore very natural for the common man not to take into account the definition of the deity as given by these sacrifice-loving latter day *Mimamsakas.* He wants his God to be real, to be supernatural and transcendental, and to be possessed at the same time of the requisite love and power to be ever near him and help him effectively.

In this way more than one of the prominent gods of the Veda began to be personally worshipped, otherwise than through the old over-formal sacrifices, gods such as Indra, Rudra, Brahma and Vishnu. We have enough evidence to indicate that many Vedic gods came to be so worshipped independently. In the course of this process some people chose one deity for their worship, while others chose other deities. Besides this, we have to take note of the fact that the Aryas who brought their Vedic religion and Aryan civilization into this land were new-comers from oùtside: and they were comparatively few in number. Before they came to this land, other people were dwelling therein whose language and civilization were different, and whose ideas and institutions were different, from those of the Aryas. These original inhabitants were, as far as we can make out with the help of available evidence—which is, however, hostile—a rather wild people who, nevertheless had a real civilization of their own, and had also an ordered social organization of their own. They were often found to be very powerful and clever in their conduct of affairs. Above all they had also a religion of their own, although this religion of theirs is declared to have been comparatively of a much lower kind than that of the Aryas. The religion that was then current among them is understood to have been characterised by the worship of the phallus, of serpents and trees and other things of that kind; and by reason of the magic and witch-craft associated therewith, it appears to have been a primitive magical religion as well. These and other primitive elements of religion must have been found to exist among the original inhabitants of India, when the Aryas came in with their comparatively higher and more potent civilization. At that time these comparatively less cultured and less civilized original inhabitants could not of course grasp the meaning and aim of the Vedic chants and of the sacrificial religion of the victorious Aryas. And the Aryan priests, who were responsible for the proper conduct of the Aryan sacrifices, considered, as it was very natural in those days, that only the Aryan people were entitled to perform those Aryan sacrifices. So the sacrificial religion of the Aryas could not easily be made to spread among the non-Aryan inhabitants of the land. In addition to this the common human tendency of these non-Aryans in favour of a personally responsive deity must have to a noticeable extent told against the fatal completion of the sacerdotal process of ceremonial fossilisation in religion.

This sort of exclusiveness in religion is nothing very strange or very peculiar in the history of human civilization. Those of you that know anything about the religion of the Jews may remember that, till a very late period in the history of Judaism, it was an exclusive religion. It was a religion to adopt which the Jews alone were, by birth, entitled, but the Gentiles were not. Later on, however, the Jews also began to take in converts to their religion: they did not, however, allow these converts to enter freely the Holy-of Holies in their temple at Jerusalem. These converts were allowed to go only as far as the gate; and for this reason they went by the name of the Proselytes of the Gate. And even this became permissible, as I told you, very late in the history of Judaism. In the earlier stages of its history, Judaism was a rigorously exclusive religion. So also, if you go to the earlier history of Rome and of Greece, you will find there the same religious exclusiveness. The religion of the Latin tribes was distinctively exclusive. Nobody, who did not belong to any one of those Latin tribes, had any right to take part in the public worship which they conducted from time to time. Among the Hellenic people of Greece also, those, who did not by birth belong to the Hellenic fraternity, were not allowed to take part in their public worship. In fact, in connection with the development of every historically evolved religion, we find that at one time, in the early stages of its evolution, it must have been exclusive. And yet the exclusiveness of the sacrificial religion of the Vedas has been, in modern days, made the theme of much harsh criticism directed against the ancient Brahmanical priests of India. The chief complaint against these priests is that they managed to keep all higher religion and higher social privileges to themselves, and that the sense of human equality was smothered by them and kept away in the region of the improper and the impossible. This is an accusation based on ignorance in relation to the exact conditions of historic evolution in religion. We have to bear in mind that, in the progress of human civilization, most early religions are characterised by exclusiveness at first. We generally start with the exclusive religion of the tribe; and this sometimes develops into the religion of a group or federation of tribes, which again may, under favourable circumstances, grow into the religion of a nation. In all these stages religion has to be largely exclusive; and it is only at last that we arrive at the universal religion. If we bear this great fact in the history of religion in mind, we may see at once how the bottom of this accusation against the ancient Aryan priests of India can be knocked off with the greatest ease.

Much of what I have said regarding early religious exclusiveness may look like a digression; but you will see that it is not without its bearing on the important question of the forces that gave rise to that universal religion, which has come to be known by the name of Vaishnavism. In the course of its natural development, religion in our country also became more and more universal; and with the growth of universalism in religion all distinctions of race, caste and creed had to disappear in the matter of men's religious eligibility for the attainment of the highest good of soul-salvation. I say advisedly that even differences of creed disappeared in this matter under the benign influence of the larger religious universalism in the country, because universal Hinduism has proved to be so comprehensively tolerant as to admit readily the title of all mankind for salvation, and to take away from life much of the unwholesome bitterness of feeling generally arising from differences in religious creed and opinion. This is a point in relation to Hinduism which can indeed be very fully demonstrated to be true.

Here, I may, in passing, point out that even so early as the time of Vasishta and Visvamitra the sympathetic and expansive tendencies of liberalism seem to have struggled to come up in the sphere of religion in India. Visvamitra was a liberal seer, even as Vasishtha was a conservative sage, who wanted the Vedic religion to be confined solely to the Aryas. That Visvamitra desired even this religion to be made universal, seems to be borne out by the well known story of Trisanku. Whether you approve of this view regarding our ancient Aryan liberalism in religion or not, this much is clear, that in later times the sacrificial religion had, in spite of its having been more or less expanded and allowed to spread, largely to disappear, partly on account of its own over-luxurious and redundant growth, and partly on account of its notable unsuitability to satisfy the earnest cravings in the heart of man after a real, hearty and living religion. And when it thus naturally faded away, we find that three deities known to the Vedas came to hold a prominent position in the popular religion of the Hindus—Rudra, Vishnu and Brahma.

With this natural decadence of the overburdened Vedic ritualism and its many and multiform sacrifices, we observe two religious forces making themselves more-

and more markedly effective and acting in consonance with each other in the evolution of further religious progress. The germs of philosophic speculation found in the Vedas grew rapidly and culminated in the production of our justly famous *Upanishads*: and the popular force in favour of the personal deity also asserted itself as against the weakened sacerdotalism of decadent Vedic ritualism. It is in fact as the result of the operation of these two forces that the idea of the Hindu trinity of gods came into existence, so as to serve well the demands of religious philosophy on the one hand, and the felt religious needs of the advancing popular mind on the other. When these gods of the trinity came to hold a prominent position in Hindu religion, even then the old spirit of the religion of the Vedas, that among the gods there is none higher and none lower, that each god as he is worshipped may well be looked upon as supreme—that spirit of *henotheism* as Max Muller called it—persisted among the thoughtful people: and with its persistence it was impossible for them to declare that any one was higher or lower among these three gods. In the meanwhile philosophy had, as I have already hinted, begun to produce more notable results than in the earlier days of the religion of the Vedas. I don't mean to say that in the Vedas we do not see the real beginnings of Hindu philosophy. It would be very wrong if I said so. On the other hand, there is ample evidence to show that potent germs of early philosophic thought are found in great abundance in the Vedas—particularly in the

Rig-Veda and in the *Atharvana-Veda*. That these germs should have grown well and produced large and highly valuable results is very natural indeed among a people so notably prone to be speculative and religious as the Hindus have been for centuries. The *Upanishads* are sometimes called the *Vedanta*, which means literally the end of the Vedas. If it is not thus literally interpreted to mean the last portion of the Vedas, it may be made to denote the aim or purpose of the Vedas, that for the attainment of which the Vedas seem to have steadily striven. Whatever the interpretation of the word *Vedanta* may be, we are able to trace in the treatises going by the name of the *Upanishads*, the sources of the later systems of Hindu philosophy known as the *Sankhya*, the *Yoga* and the *Vedanta* systems. Even Buddhistic and Jaina philosophy are held by some to be traceable to them. Those treatises themselves do not give any definite expression to any particular system of philosophy. They are not the work of one mind like the systems of modern philosophers, such as Kant, Hegel, Mill, or Spencer. Although not systematised as in modern philosophic works, the thoughts in them are strikingly luminous, often very piercingly and gloriously luminous. These thoughts take us to the farthest limit of all philosophy and impel us to go even beyond, and are expressed in language which is most enthralling and highly sublime. I believe my philosophic friends will support me, if I say that, after all, there is much deadening influence in system-making. As soon as we put together our philosophic thoughts into a system, there is a natural tendency for that system to lose spontaniety and originality and to become lifeless and hidebound. They lose their power to expand, and the germs of originality in them become crushed under the great pressure of the mechanical forces of systematisation. Luckily, therefore, for us, the authors of the *Upanishads* were not like modern philosophers: they did not endeavour to build up systems. They must have felt that their function as teachers was simply to give free expression to what they from time-to-time saw like seers. They left system-making to their later and weaker followers. That is why we have had in this country a profuse growth of pure and highly aspiring philosophy out of our *Upanishads*—of philosophy which has flourished in various forms and under various names, and has been systematised in various ways by various scholars and sages and saints.

Among the systems of philosophy that arose out of the luminous thoughts of the *Upanishads*, the very first was in all probability the *Sankhya* system of Kapila, which is considered by Brahminical tradition also to be one of the oldest systems of orthodox Hindu philosophy. Then came the *Yoga* sytem; and later on still, by combining, as I believe, the *Sankhya* and the *Yoga* together, came the *Vedanta* system. And when these systematised philosophies began to flourish, they too had of course their part to play in shaping the growth of religion and in modifying the general conception of God among the people. I told you that, in response to the inevitable cravings of the human heart, the sacrificial religion of the Vedas had to be set aside in favour of a religion wherein there was a God who was a real support to the worshipper, a God with whom the worshipper could take refuge, and from whom the worshipper could obtain love and help in times of trial and hardship. I also said that, among the Vedic gods, three came to occupy prominently the personal position which the human heart required that its gods should occupy: and these are Brahma, Vishnu and Siva. In the early days of the origin of this Hindu Trinity, the old henotheistic idea was evidently operating powerfully enough to prevent any such differentiation in rank among these gods, as later controversy brought into existence in later times so as to embitter the religious feelings of the Hindus very much. Such a differentiation in rank between Vishnu and Siva, for instance, we don't see much of, even about the time when our famous poet Kalidasa flourished. In dealing with these three gods, Kalidasa looks upon them as though they were very nearly equal, and shows no kind of partiality to any one deity at the expense of another, although there is very good reason to believe that he was himself a worshipper of Siva. When he happens to offer his prayers to Siva, he offers them as to the Supreme Deity; and when again he has to offer prayers to Vishnu, he offers them similarly as if to the Supreme Deity: and the language of philosophic description and praise he applies to Vishnu in one place is almost identical with the language of adoration he applies to Siva in another place. And he honours Brahma almost equally with these two gods. But how long is it possible for this religion of the equal Trinity to go on unchanged? How can you have three gods, and consider each of them to be Supreme? It is inevitable for a question like this to arise after the mind begins to philosophise a little. If you do not philosophise—the god whom you for the time being consider to be supreme—your heart naturally goes forth in adoration to that god; and in his worship, you forget everything else. But if you philosophise, you are led to become more and more circumspect. In such circumspection there is both safety and danger: and philosophical circumspection made the later attitude of India one of inquisitive doubt regarding this equal position of the *Trimurtis*. What I have called philosophical circumspection made it in fact necessary that the assumed position of equality among the gods of the Hindu Trinity must be accounted for in some reasonable manner. Thus there was naturally an apportionment of functions to these gods; and all the three gods making up the *Trimurtis* were held to be different and partial manifestations of the one great God of advancing Hindu philosophy. Thus Brahma became the creator, and Vishnu the sustainer, and Siva the destroyer.

Why is that one of these gods came to be looked upon as creator, another as sustainer, and the third as destroyer? We have to note here firstly the effect of the germinal force underlying the ancient conception of these gods. The word *Brahman* is often used to denote the Vedic prayer that is offered to Vedic deities. Such Vedic prayer has been personified as a deity, and declared to be powerful enough even to create. This conception of *Brahman* in the Veda resembles in many respects the Greek idea of the Logos. The relation between language and the meaning underlying language has played a great part in the development of Hindu philosophic thought, particularly in the matter of explaining the relation between the visible universe and the invisible reality that is behind it. Often enough we find Indian philosophers saying that the visible universe is something like the audible world of language; and that the invisible foundation of the universe is like the power of meaning possessed by language—the power of meaning which we cannot perceive with any of the senses. The relation between the word and its meaning has indeed been long held by our thinkers to be representative of the relation between the phenomenal universe and the reality which is behind it, forming its enduring basis and everlasting support. That is indeed one of the noticeable ways in which we find higher Indian thought growing, developing and expanding. Moreover, in Vedic literature, in the *Upanishads* in particular, we have it stated that the Creator willed, and thereby created the world. If you will, how do you give expression to your will? You do so either by means of the language you speak, or by means of the deed you do. Hence the language, which gives expression to the will of the speaker, may well become identified with the will itself. And when the creating will is seen to be really responsible for the creation of the universe, we may very well maintain that it is the word, which gives expression to the will, that is responsible for such creation. Hence the expression बहु स्याम्, being representative of the will of the Creator, naturally came to be recognised as the immediate cause of the production of creation. If we understand that the idea underlying *Brahman* is distinctly that of the 'word', and if we also bear in mind the relation between the word and its meaning, as well as the relation between the will and the word which gives expression to it, we may very easily realise how natural it is for the idea of creation to become associated with the Vedic *Brahman*. Thus arose Brahma the creator in the Trinity; and philosophy also differentiated and assigned to him the function of creation.

Now how about Siva? He is, as you have been informed, the Vedic god Rudra, and as such the god of fire—Agni. This Agni as Rudra is declared in Vedic literature to have a *santta tanuh* and also a *ghoratanuh*—a form which is lovely and peaceful and a form which is terrific and fierce. In the fierce form which he has, we have to look upon him as a destroyer; and a destroying god becomes naturally the punisher of faithlessness and evil-doing. Such a god can be considered neither strange nor unwanted among the essential elements of a complete religion. In this universe of ours, we may see the processes of creation, sustentation and destruction always going on side by side. We surely cannot think of the world as being at any time free from decay; if we could do that, the world would certainly cease to be what it is. I don't know if there is any poet who can command a sufficiently strong and clear imagination to portray the condition of the world as altogether unassociated with destruction and dissolution. If destruction disappear from the midst of the world, there would be no room in it at all for renovation. And will not most young men protest against such a situation? The stage of the world would then be quite fully occupied by very superfluous veterans; and when the world's stage becomes so overburdened with exhausted veterans, the young men can surely have no scope there for life and for growth. Naturally the condition of the world would then be very different—so different indeed as to be quite incapable of being consistently conceived. Destruction is thus an essential element in the universe as we know it. Whether it is possible to have a universe without destruction and decay therein, is a question which we deed not at present discuss; for we know only one universe, and there can be no good at all in troubling ourselves about the possibility or otherwise of another way of organising another universe. Let us take into consideration the one only universe which we know—that, wherein we have to live from day to day, even as we have to die when the hour for it comes: and this universe is characterised by decay and destruction. Destruction is as essential a part therein as creation and sustentation are. Hence—to whom this essential function of destruction is to be assigned—is a question which philosophy has every right to ask. And the fierce Rudra as Siva came to be recognised as the most competent god to take upon himself the responsibility for performing this function of destruction in the universe.

Then there is the work of sustentation to be performed and looked after in the universe. Some god must take care of that work. With the idea underlying the conception of god Vishnu, there came to be the association, as you know, of the idea of the Bhagavat. There had thus come into existence the conception of a god as an all-pervading source of light and life, of a god who, occupying the supremest position in the universe, is ever helpful to mankind as the bestower of beneficial powers and gifts and blessings on them. As Vishnu became such a god, it was quite natural that he was made responsible for looking after the work of sustentation in the universe. In the midst of the birth, decay and death, which are everywhere evident in the universe, we also see that things endure in a more or less marked condition of steady well-being for shorter or longer intervals of time. It is this endurance of things in the condition of comparative well-being that has been designated as sustentation. And the god, who has to look after such a function of sustentation, must obviously be a god of love. The creating god Brahma has merely to deal out the barest justice to all beings in accordance with the law of *karma*. The importance of this function of Brahma in the universe cannot at all be gainsaid; but his function is not designed to make him a suitable object of either religious fear or religious love. In the manner in which the fierce Rudra became quite appropriately the destroying god and an object of religious fear to his worshippers, Vishnu became equally appropriately the protecting god and an object of religious love to his worshippers. Siva, as the austere god of fear and unrelenting rigour could easily become Mahadeva or the 'great god' among the people. But Vishnu alone could be always *Santakara*, full of peace and benignity, so as to love his worshippers and be really loved by them in return.

In this way the functions of the three gods of the Hindu Trinity became distributed among them. At any rate I can offer no better explanation of why Brahma became the creator, Rudra the destroyer, and Vishnu the protector. Old Vedic tradition and comparatively later philosophic thought thus gave rise to the religion of the *Trimurtis.* This religion was, however, from the very beginning lacking in the element of finality even for the time being, as its three gods were looked upon as mere functional aspects of the one only God of the universe, the God of all gods. It is the tendency of the aspiration of religion to look up always, and to endeavour to rise to higher and higher levels of worship and realisation. Therefore, after conceiving the one only God of the universe, in whom there has to be the natural and final synthesis of all the other gods, the heart of the worshipper cannot be at ease, if he is ever called upon to worship any being who is in any manner less than the sublime and almighty fulness of his one only God, the God of all gods. Siva and Vishnu, who had already become popular gods, rose under this impulse to represent the one only God of true philosophy, inasmuch as popular imagination and its predilections and prejudices would not very naturally be in favour of the adoption of an entirely new deity to represent this one only God of philosophy. Indeed Saivism and Vaishnavism appear in this light in the *Mahabharata*, although we cannot fail to notice therein a very marked tendency in favour of looking upon Vishnu as the one only God of true philosophy. It is true that our great poet Kalidasa was not a narrowly sectarian bigot in his worship of Siva as the Supreme God; but we cannot therefore say that he was unaware of Vaishnavism as an independent religion in which Vishnu happened to be the Supreme God. By the time the gradual growth of the *Mahabharata* came to its end, Saivism and Vaishnavism had already assumed their distinctive shapes, and had come to be accepted among the people as different forms of one and the same religion derived from the same scriptural and philosophic sources.

In the meanwhile, that is, in the interval between the grand climacteric of *Upanishadic* thought and the culmination of the age-long growth of the *Mahabharata*, a new force of great significance came into existence in the religious and social atmosphere of Indian civilization; and that is none other than the momentous force of Buddhism. Buddhism was really a revolt against the overdone sacerdotalism of the Vedic sacrificial religion of the Brahmins. Probably it was also a revolt against the aristocratic isolation of the Brahminical priests and their monopoly to serve as the clergy, that is, as authorised teachers of religion and philosophy. When a revolt against any established order of institutions is started, it is found, in the history of all countries and civilizations, that the revolt as revolt invariably goes too far. Indeed the process is comparable to the oscillation of the pendulum in this respect: men first go to one extreme in one direction, and then they go to the other extreme in the opposite direction. Since Buddhism operated as a revolt againt the excesses of Brahminical sacredotalism and clerical monopoly, Gautama the Buddha tried to establish beyond doubt that he was as much entitled to be a teacher of religion as any Brahmin born, and taught that the mechanical religion of over-formal ceremonialism and life-taking sacrifices does nothing more than merely cause unjustifiable injury to innocent animal life. He felt sincerely that such a religion cannot purify a man's life, cannot satisfy the deep spiritual longings of his heart, and cannot make his life's burden of sorrows and sufferings lighter or his hope of final freedom and salvation surer and more cheerful. In accordance with the tendency of the age, the Buddhistic revolt itself had to be based upon and guided by philosophic speculation; and the philosophy on which it was accordingly based is now recognized by most scholars to have been derived from the luminous and inspiring thoughts contained in the *Upanishads*, and probably also from some of the later systems of philosophy built up with their aid. We have both *Sankhya* and *Yoga* elements in Buddhistic philosophy, and also a large number of ideas and doctrines directly traceable to the *Upanishads*. The most notable feature in Buddhistic philosophy is that it does not cause men to trouble themselves about the question of the final philosophic reality. It does not ask—"Is there a God, and if there is, what is His relation to the universe?" This aspect of philosophy, Buddhism purposely ignored. It started with the proposition that life in this world is ever full of sorrow and pain and misery, and that to get out of such a life of grief and pain and misery once for all, so as to go back to it no more, has to be the chief purpose of life—its very *summum bonum*.

How is this purpose to be accomplished? The problem is one of practical ethics, and its solution was found out to be in the annihilation of *trishna*—of the thirsting after the pleasing objects of the senses and the agreeable delights of life. It is this *trishna* or thirsting after the pleasing things of life which is declared to be really responsible for the bondage of life—I won't say, for the bondage of the soul, because the question of the soul appears to have been left undecided in Buddhism. If we get rid of this *trishna*, we get rid of bondage; and then we become free. And what becomes of us when we so become free. We attain *nirvana* as the Buddhishts say. But Buddhistic *nirvana* is not in all respects the same as the Hindu salvation of *moksha*. On the attainment of *nirvana*, man's continuously recurring mundane life of pain, sorrow and misery—of birth, growth and decay and death—is declared to disappear altogether. What there will be after all this misery disappears, Buddha does not want people to enquire into and examine. His ideal lay altogether in practical ethical life. "Look to the ethical life, don't waste your time in vain metaphysical wranglings regarding the nature of the *Brahman* or the destiny of the soul "—he is known to have declared more than once. Whether the soul is real, whether it is something separate and apart from or the same as God, he did not care to consider. These discussions are, after all, such as cannot lead to anything like really final and irrebuttable conclusions. Indeed we cannot satisfactorily solve these metaphysical problems and give to their solutions the character of finality. Philosophy would cease to be philosophy if there were to be real finality about all its conclusions: and Buddha obviously thought that this absence of finality made metaphysical discussions useless for the practical guidance of life. There may or may not be a *Brahman*, and this *Brahman* may or may not be related to the universe. We may or may not have a soul that remains and endures even after the attainment of *nirvana*. These problems were to him practically insignificant. His concern evidently was to free human life from the net of over-wrought metaphysics as much as from the redundant overgrowth of ritualism, and to make it practically pure, blissful and serene. Such is a brief statement of the more important aims of Buddhism. You may see here how, in his revolt, Buddha went to the other extreme. It is true he has not denied God. He has not denied the soul either. But he has distinctly told all those that seek guidance from him that there is no good in trying to solve problems about God and the soul, and that ceremonial worship and sacrifice as elements of religion and aids to conduct are very much worse than meaningless mockery.

That is how Buddha's work came to figure in the field of Indian religion, and he naturally interfered with the even progress of old Hindu thought. He had therefore to be met. After Buddha, his followers laboured with exemplary zeal to make his religion spread. Although they took much sincere and earnest trouble, their work, like that of all propagandistic workers, made them indulge rather freely in that kind of low activity, in which their chief aim turned out to be not so much to spread the good teachings of Buddha in regard to the necessity of making human life here on earth pure, unselfish, holy and helpful, as to see that other religions were subjected to harsh criticism and were made to lose their influence in the world. They, therefore, freely found fault with the ancient Vedic religion of the Hindus. Some of the old criticisms of the Buddhists are even now repeated by other modern critics of Hindu religion and Hindu scriptures. The attempt to meet these criticisms in earnest gave rise to a religious revival among the Hindus. In the case of this revival of Hinduism also, the process was indeed like the oscillation of the pendulum. When Buddhism went to one extreme, the Brahminical revival went to the other. When Hinduism started afresh to assert itself against Buddhistic opposition, it was the *Mimamsaka* who at first came forward to vindicate the Hindu religion. He relied upon and worked for establishing the infallible authority of the Vedas. According to him the Vedas are self-produced and eternal, they are not the result of any inspired vision of any seer, they are not even revelation which is limited in time; but they are eternal and self-existent, they have always been and will ever be. With the aid of such an eternal, self-existent and infallible Veda, it was his aim not so much to establish any form of theistic ethics and rational religious worship, as to resuscitate the nearly dead ritualism of the old Vedic religion with its many and multiform sacrifices. That was the position which the *Mimamsaka* held. It was on this ground that he took his stand against the Buddhist. But we know that such a position, resting solely upon the eternality and infallible authority of the Vedas, cannot be made to tell effectively against the purely ethical practical position taken up by the great humanitarian teacher Buddha. When the argument of the *Mimamsaka* against his Buddhistic critics could not thus have the desired effect in rehabilitating Hinduism, then there arose the necessity of meeting philosophy by philosophy and ethics by ethics. This could be done quite easily, because the human heart cannot go on for ever in pleased satisfaction with a religion that does not take God into consideration, and does not take the soul and its final destiny into consideration. The religion that entirely relies upon a more or less empirically determined discipline of ethical conduct in life, must be, from the very nature of the case, an unsatisfying religion. My learned and esteemed friend in the chair will, I am sure, corroborate me when I give expression to the view that the true foundation of all enduring ethics has to be found in metaphysics. That ethics which is not founded upon metaphysics is certain to be shaky ethics. That is what I understand all true philosophy to teach. That is also what the human heart evidently feels from its very bottom. It is all very well to say that our lives must be pure, and unselfish and sinless. But why should they be so? We are all prone to know the better and do the worse. As St. Paul has put it, there is a double nature in every one of us. There is a certain something in us which always prompts us to do that which is right and good; and there is also a certain something else in us which prompts us to do what is not right and good. Between these two prompting forces in the heart of man—there is a struggle going on incessantly. If, in the course of this constant struggle, the force prompting us to do the right is not supported strongly by religion and by philosophy, then naturally the force which prompts us to do the wrong will overpower us and make our lives altogether faulty and unworthy.

Even with the aid of the support derived from the helping hand of philosophy and religion, do not so many of us give way before the force which always tempts us to do evil? Therefore this purely ethical, and agnostic and empirical religion could not satisfy all the religious cravings of the human heart. It could not uphold religion and morality so sufficiently or so completely rationally as to make them stand on their own legs and enable us to declare with the unfailing authority of reality that the life of righteousness is alone for ever and ever the proper life for man.

Accordingly, it became necessary that the religion which strove from a theistic standpoint to counteract the agnostic influence of Buddhism, should address itself to the work of making the authoritative commandment and justification of morality and unselfishness more satisfactory than Buddhism could ever prove them to be. The work of the *Mimamsakas* in establishing the divine authority of the Vedas and their everlasting character could not, as we have seen, give rise to this result. And so something else had to be done to bring about such a result, and thereby establish the high value and worthiness of Hindu scriptures and Hindu tradition in vindicating morality and in satisfying all the high spiritual requirements of religion. This work had necessarily to be done; and it was taken up by Sankaracharya in right earnest. That such was the need of the hour had been made out by the famous Gaudapadacharya even before the time of Sankara. Indeed Gaudapada had already succeeded in formulating a scheme of thought whereby the humanitarian ethics of Buddhism might very well be evolved out of the *Upanishadic* metaphysics of Hinduism. Many of us are not conscious of the manner in which we are hour after hour moulded by our environments; and often enough we feel that we are absolutely free agents in all that we think and do. But if we carefully examine the processes of history with a view to find out why it is that in one and the same country the leading men of one age think in one manner, while those of another age think in a different manner, we are sure to find out that there are natural forces which tend to produce such variations in thought and aim. It is in consequence of these forces that they think and act as they do in history. If we bear this well in mind, we may quite easily discern how very unconsciously Gaudapada and Sankara must have adopted the line of reasoning they did, for the purpose of over-coming the unwholesome sceptic effects of the agnosticism of the Buddhists. One of the chief ends to be gained in this conflict was the establishment of the authority of the Vedas, which meant the same thing as the establishment of the authoritativeness of the old long-cherished religious thoughts and traditions of the country. Another such object was to derive that same purity and sinlessness and selflessness of life, as was advocated by Buddha, from the teachings of our old Vedic and Vedantic religion. These are indeed among the practcal historical results of the philosophical doctrines taught by Sankaracharya.

During his all too short a period of life, his thoughts as a philosopher and his work as a religious reformer produced very marked and momentous results. While accepting the *Mimamsaka's* views regarding the eternality and infallibility of the sacred scriptures of the Hindus, Sankara had to contend against his exaggerated faith in the sacerdotal ceremonialism of the Vedas. There is very good evidence to show that he fought this fight with very remarkable success. On the strength of the eternality and infallibility of the Vedas, he had further to establish that the agnostic ethics and humanitarianism of Buddhism, though very high in their then moral value, were really inferior to Vedantic ethics and Vedantic humanitarianism. How well he accomplished this, the later history of Buddhism in India abundantly demonstrates. In the course of his endeavour to re-establish Hinduism unshakably on its ancient foundations, he of course worked most nobly and heroically for purity as well as unity in human life and human society.

If he had lived longer he might have given us much more of the treasure of his thoughts, and might have enlightened many more dark corners in the great field of Indian philosophy and Hindu religious aspiration. And yet, what he did in the short span of his life is more than enough to immortalize him a thousand times. His great success in carrying out the object, which he obviously had in view, is evident from the fact that his teachings put an end to the effective opposition of Buddhism against Hinduism, and promoted in a notable manner the forward progress of Hinduism along the lines of a highly improved ethical universalism. His object was evidently to win back those pious and earnest and thoughtful people, who had strayed away from the old fold of Hindu religious tradition and Hindu philosophic thought. Consequently Sankaracharya's religion had to be based on the philosophical foundation of the higher pantheistic monism; and it thus became pre-eminently the religion of *jnanin*. His teaching is, as you know, that the Supreme *Brahman* is identical with the soul, and that everything in the phenomenal universe is an illusory manifestation of that *Brahman* who is in fact the one only reality. Such being the position of Sankaracharya, he had naturally to propound highly metaphysical problems and theories, and had to prove that the soul is in fact a part of this one great reality in the universe, and that becoming absorbed into it in the end is indeed the great salvation of *moksha*. When that aim of becoming absorbed into *Brahman* is accomplished, souls get out of the bondage of *samsara* at once and as a matter of course; and in this state of *moksha*, every soul comes to its own enjoyment of unlimited light and eternal bliss and peace. It is not difficult to make out how these teachings of his tend to give a firmer and more rational metaphysical foundation even for Buddhistic ethics. In this we have the greatest historical achievement to be placed to the credit of Sankaracharya. He saw, and made others also see distinctly, that the moral fruits of pure Buddhistic life were more fully capable of being derived from Vedantic Hinduism. When this became evident, how could Buddhistic critics decry any longer the old religion of the Hindus with justice? When before Sankaracharya the *Mimamsaka* had worked effectively to establish the eternal and infallible character of the Vedas, and when Sankaracharya later on demonstrated the high ethical value and humanitarian purpose of the teachings contained in those same Vedas, the position of the religion of the Hindus, as found upon their ancient scriptures, became altogether impregnable. It certainly cannot be amiss to point out here that there is very good evidence in the writings of Sankaracharya to indicate that he was himself an ardent Vaishnava: he may well be made out to have been a great Bhagavata. Although his achievements in relation to the great work of strengthening the philosophical fortifications of Vedantic Hinduism have been comprehensively general and non-sectarian in character, it is abundantly clear that he must have felt that his higher pantheistic monism was in no way seriously incompatible with Vaishnavism even in its form as the accepted religion of the ancient Bhagavatas.

It has, however, to be observed that the large body of the Hindus in the country could not easily comprehend Sankaracharya's Vedantic religion, since it was too philosophical for the common human mind. The common man could not indeed derive sufficient religious satisfaction from it. His need even then was to have a God who would love him, who would come to help him and render protection unto him whenever he got into difficulties—a God at whose feet he might throw himself unreservedly so that He in His divine wisdom might do with him whatever He chose. The sense of man's dependence upon God, his instinct of love to God, and his felt need for an always unfailing divine support could not be easily satisfied by the sublimely impersonal God of Sankara's pantheistic monism. What wonder, if soon afterwards there arose among the people the desire to see where else they could obtain their religious satisfaction ? The old religion of the Hindus was distinctly marked by the supreme dominance of a loving and saving divine personality in it. Even before Buddhism there was, as it appears, the religion of the Hindu Trinity. And after Buddhism lost its great influence in India, the popular position of Vedantic Hinduism became very highly improved. This religion had by that time been proved to be in no way inferior to Buddhism or any other religion, in the matter of establishing the obligatoriness of pure ethical conduct as based on sinlessness and selflessness in life. And yet the need was felt for a personal God, and for a more emotional and less intellectual religion than that of Sankara. This more emotional and less intellectual religion had in fact been known well to the people of India before. Such a religion is clearly traceable in the pages of the *Mahabharata* and in the *Puranas*. And after Buddhis and Sankaracharya, this old emotional religion was felt to be more and more wanted. Accordingly religious reformers arose and came forward to supply the felt need of the hour. Among those who so arose in India to give this needed emotional turn to the re-established and freshly progressive Hindu religion, Ramanuja-charya certainly played a very important part, and produced very notable results as a fearless and faithful worker in the field of Hindu religious and social reform. There have been others who also endeavoured in their days to do this kind of work; but among all such, Ramanujacharya may be made out to have been undeniably the most famous and fruitful worker. Ramanujacharya had, of course, his predecessors, who had prepared the way for him, as the history of the Sri-Vaishnava religion distinctly shows. And in carrying out this requisite reform in Hindu religion, that is, in making it a religion of loving devotion to an all-powerful and all-merciful God, what Ramanuja mainly did was that he combined the old religious views of the Bhagavatas with the Vedantic ideas of Sankara's higher pantheism, so as to make his *advaita* or absolute non-dualism become *visishtadvaita* or qualified non-dualism. Ramanuja's aim was evidently to emphasise the religious value of devotion and service and self-surrender to God, but not to make the realization of the oneness of God with the soul of man and with the universe the basis for moral conduct, and the means for the attainment of the sublime salvation of *moksha*. The need for moral conduct, for purity, for sinlessness, and for selflessness in life has been believed in and proclaimed by all great religious teachers in India as in every other part of the world. But they have differed as to the question of how this sinless life is to be realised in practice. Is it to be made dependent upon spiritual and philosophical realisation, or is it to be made dependent upon the culture of the tender and benevolent emotions, has in fact been the practical problem at issue. There can be no doubt that both the processes are capable of yielding the fine fruit of pure and noble conduct. However to most men and women the culture of the emotions happens to be easier than the achievement of spiritual and philosophic realisation.

Ramanujacharya accordingly declared *bhakti* to be the most suitable means to achieve purity, sinlessness, and selflessness in life; and hence this same *bhakti* was according to him the truest and the most unfailing means for the attainment of the salvation of *moksha*. The emotion of *bhakti* is said to be a feeling akin to love; it is indeed deep devotion and love. Even in our common daily life, we may very well realize what a potent factor love is in encouraging morality, and in establishing purity and selflessness and sinlessness in life. Imagine a young man who is entirely absorbed in himself, who does not care to think of anybody or anything other than himself,—imagine further that, either as in India or in the fashion of Europeans, he marries a beautiful and worthy damsel, and becomes day after day more and more attached to her in love. Suppose this young man of the above description goes to the Bangalore fruit-market and sees rows of fine luscious fruits exposed for sale there. His mouth of course waters, and he buys some choice fruits among them. Does he eat them himself? He would probably have done so in those old self-centred days of his uniquely single blessedness. He does not and cannot do so now; for his love to his wife is so true and so deep that although at the very sight of the fruits his own mouth profusely watered, he carries them home to his wife and gives them to her in preference to himself. And if in course of time he becomes the father of a number of children, and then goes again to the same market and sees similar fruits, his mouth probably will not then water at all. He will have by that time become too much of an altruist, that is, too much of a true lover of others, and his mouth will surely have learnt not to water on seeing even the best of fruits. Nevertheless, he is certain to buy the fruits, in the belief that those fruits will be even more delicious and agreeable to his children than they were to him in those old days when his mouth freely and fearlessly watered in his own interest at the sight of the sweet fruits. He buys them and takes them home. To whom does he give them now? Evidently not to his wife, who is now to him no more than the worthy and respectable mother of his dear children. But he gives them to the children. This clearly shows how potent love is in expanding our sympathies and in killing our selfishness. And by killing selfishness, we in fact kill all that is calculated to encourage sinfulness and impurity in us. With the disappearance of selfishness, every temptation that tends to make our lives unrighteous and faulty disappears at once. In this way love may be made out to be a very potent factor in giving rise to purity and unselfishness in life. If this feeling of love is steadily and carefully cultivated in the human heart, if it is made to find its object not merely in the wife and the children, but in that great Being, who is the very life and foundation of the universe, and from whom comes all that is good and true and beautiful in the universe, if that Being is made the object of our love, then there will arise, as they put it in Sanskrit, *anuragadviragah*—that is, through intense attachment to that divine Being, there will arise in us absolute non-attachment to ourselves.

This idea is sometimes illustrated in Hindu literature by taking the example of an uncontrollable illegitimate attachment which a man may have to a mistress, although he is morally bound to bestow on his own wedded wife all his love and attachment. As his illegitimate love grows in intensity, that is, as the object of his illegitimate love becomes more and more dear to him, his lawfully wedded wife may be seen to be discarded by him more and more. Thus his *viraga* or want of attachment to the wedded wife bears an inverse ratio to his *anuraga* or loving attachment to the illegitimate mistress. This example is not a very happy one morally: nevertheless as an illustration it is very telling. And what I want you to understand from it is, that, if we make God the object of all our attachment, then everything else ceases in time to have the power of attracting our love. With the growth of such a full God-love in us, our love of pleasure, of wealth, of beauty and of power disappears like mist before the rising sun. The only love that then endures is our love of God. And the full import of this God-love depends upou our conception of God. If it be realised that everything that is in the universe has come from Him, and in due time goes back to Him—if such is the conception which we have of God, then, when He becomes the object of our love, all His creatures also become the objects of our love as a matter of course. How will it be possible for us to live a life of selfishness, when God and all his creatures have thus become the objects of our true and devoted love? Such a thing is indeed impossible. We cannot love God and His creatures sincerely, and love also at the same time our own sweet little selves. The love of man's sweet little self fades away in the larger presence of the love of God and His creatures. Here, therefore, is an efficient and worthy means placed at the disposal of man, by which he may overcome his tendencies in favour of selfishness and sinfulness—and that means is man's loving devotion to God, which is in Hinduism known by the name of *bhakti.* Here also *anuraga* or loving attachment to God and all His creatures gives rise to *viraga* or the feeling of non-attachment in relation to one's self. It is not merely that love expands our sympathies and kills our selfishness: love indeed does more—it stimulates in us self-sacrifice and impels us to wear ourselves away cheerfully in serving those whom we love. Our love of God—when it is indeed real and hearty—is fully capable of turning us into earnest and sincere servants of all His creatures. In fact it is in serving His creatures that our love of God finds its satisfaction and makes itself alive and visible. And it is actually maintained in the Sri-Vaishnavism of Ramanuja that to love and honour and serve the Bhagavatas is even more meritorious than to worship the Bhagavat. Loving devotion to God has been and is undoubtedly a great moral force in human history.

Thus with the aid of *bhakti* we may annihilate selfishness, and thereby realise *moksha*. The obligatoriness of *bhakti* is, therefore, an unfailing authority in favour of pure ethical conduct and high nobility of purpose: it is indeed an unfailing means to help us always to attain real success in living the righteous life. Moreover it is easier for us to command *bhakti* than to obtain that transcendental spiritual wisdom and the realisation of the unity of reality which Sankaracharya's philosophy demands of all its followers. The tendency to love is altogether natural and is implanted in the heart of all persons. There is in fact no person of any kind who has not a natural aptitude to love and to be moved by love. The only point to be attended to in respect of this natural emotion of love is to make it expand so widely and so comprehensively that it may have the great God Himself and all His creatures for its object. And the tendency of love to have itself lavished upon the beloved is very frequently seen to be against the conception of absolute oneness between the lover and his beloved. The function of philosophy consists largely in realising the untiy of reality, while that of *bhakti* or the emotion of God-love and divine devotion is in the realisation of union through service and self-sacrifice. When it is found that the path of *bhakti* leads the devotees of God more easily and more naturally to the attainment of *moksha* through the realised relation of God-union, than the path of wisdom or *jnana* does through the realisation of oneness with God, then as a matter of course the easier path of *bhakti* will be followed by many so as to make it become the really popular road of religious aspiration and attainment. Ramanujacharya, whose aim obviously was to make as many as possible come under the saving influence of God-love as comprehended in Vaishnavism, made *bhakti* the basis of all religious life; and to him *jnana* itself came to mean the same thing as *thakti*. In fact it is in this light that he has interpreted the *Vedanta-Sutras* of Badarayana. Accordingly, making *bhakti* as before the pivot of popular religion was one of the most important points in the life-work of Ramanujacharya. It is fully worthwhile nothing here that the Sanskrit words *bhaga*, *bhagavat*, and *bhakti* are all of the same origin etymologically; and it cannot therefore be an altogether unfounded assumption to hold that the word *bhakti* must have, almost from the very commencement of its religious history in the Sanskrit language, meant the means of worshipping Bhagavat in the spirit of true love and devotion as the one

Supreme Lord, the God of all gods. There is other evidence also to prove that the doctrine of *bhakti* is undoubtedly an ancient element in the religion of the Bhagavatas. Anyhow there can be no doubt that the all-pervading and all-enlivening Vishnu, who, as Bhagavat, is the loving bestower of all auspicious boons and blessings, and is, as Narayana, the abode of all life and the internal controller—*antaryamin*—of all beings, is most appropriately approached through *bhakti*. The most glorious delight of love is ever in experiencing the response of love to love. Therefore to a loving God, what can be more delightful than the confident and trustful love with which His devotees respond to His love? And is not Vishnu, the bestower of light and life and of all auspicious boons and blessings, a loving God? When we think of our own unworthiness to be the objects of His love, and contrast it with His infinite benevolence and the immense value of all His divine gifts, how can we conceive Him to be other than a realy loving God? On the certainty of His all-merciful and omnipotent love is based another doctrine of the Sri-Vaishnavas, which is closely allied to the doctrine of *bhakti* and may even be said to be a natural development of it. I refer to the doctrine of *prapatti* or absolute self-surrender to God, which is also spoken of sometimes as *saranagati*. This doctrine of self-surrender is based mainly on the last teaching given by Sri-Krishna to Arjuna in the *Bhagavadgita*, and it is hence held to be as authoritative as the *Gita* itself. I told you a little while ago that there are some modern philosophers also who maintain that man's sense of dependence on a higher power has to be an essential element in all religions. Whether it really has to be so or not, we need not discuss now. But it is evident that the doctrine of *prapatti* is based on such a sense of dependence on God—a dependence which is complete and unquestioningly trustful. Ramanuja's views regarding this doctrine come out most beautifully from his *Saranagatigadya*, which is a highly pathetic prayer in Sanscrit prose embodying his great faith in God as his sole refuge and only Saviour.

There is another point in the work of Ramanuja in connection with Vaishnavism, which is brought prominently to view by the name Sri-Vaishnavism, which has been given to the religion he taught and upheld. It is sometimes called Vaishnavism of the *Sri-sampradaya*. Ramanuja's religion has been called Sri-Vaishnavism, because Sri, that is, the goddess Lakshmi, is made to have an important function to perform in it. When man, by means of his *bhakti*, endeavours to attain *moksha*, it is found that he often feels helpless and hopelessly forlorn on account of his knowledge of his own culpable unworthiness to be blessed with the salvation of soul-emancipation and God-attainment as also on account of his very natural conception of God as a just and impartial apportioner of the fruits of *karma* to all His creatures. When we deal with a great question of religion and morality like the fitness of God's creatures to be saved and lifted out of the thraldom of *samsara*, and base its solution on our metaphysical conceptions of God and of the will of God, we cannot help thinking of Him as a hard task-master, who is systematically bent upon seeing that all His commandments are duly obeyed by all His creatures, and that His will is always honoured by them as law. With such an absolutely just God, who is very rightly and very naturally apt to become deeply disappointed with us whenever we violate His commandments, our chances of attaining salvation are indeed infinitely small. When we calmly measure our own capacity to conduct our lives in complete consonance with the will of God, the result is certain to fill us all with great despondency. Since the moral law is based upon the will of God, we are all bound to live our lives in accordance with the moral law. But when the weakness that is in us unnerves us and we become a prey to temptations, how can we then manage to live the life that is morally faultless? And if we break down under the heavy pressure of trying temptations, are we thereafter to have no hope of any kind regarding the attainment of the bliss of soul-salvation? In this manner we are led to face the old problem of how the mercy of the loving God may be reconciled with the strict impartiality of the absolutely just God. It is in a situation like this that we naturally feel the need for the kindly interposition of a suitable intermediary between us and our great God,—an intermediary, who on the one hand is willing and able to excuse our faults and can on the other hand effectively approach our almighty God with the petition for mercy in behalf of His weak and erring creatures. It is not here in India alone that the help of such an intermediary has been sought by pious and God-fearing people. Other religions also than this Sri-Vaishnavism seek and postulate an interceder between God and man, between the ever-just and almighty God and the weak and erring human being, so that this weak and erring being may be made to have the full benefit of divine mercy. Some make their religious *Guru* such an interceder; others, like the Christians, make a divine incarnation serve as such an interceder; and Sri-Vaishnavism looks upon Lakshmi, the divine Mother of the Universe, as such an interceder. To bear well and without harm the burden of moral and religious responsibility belonging to weak and erring mankind, some such interceder between the judging God and the human beings to be judged is very rightly recognised to be necessary by more than one well-known religion. Now in the religion taught by Ramanujacharya, this interceder is, as you have been already told, the goddess Lakshmi. The conception of Lakshmi as the divine consort of Vishnu is also an old one in Hindu religion. It is known to later Vedic literature, and has a philosophical meaning underlying it—this meaning being nothing other than the true representation of the relation between *prakriti* and *Parama-purusha*. *Prakriti* is conceived to be the wife of God, who is the Supreme Being. According to what is called by some *Pauranika Sankhya*—which is the same as the *Sankhya* of Kapila, with the exception that, in the *Pauranika Sankhya*, a Supreme Soul is postulated anu made to have the same relation to the universe as a whole as the various individual souls have to their repective embodiments—according, to this *Pauranika Sankhya*, it is maintained that *prakriti*, which is in fact the source of the created universe, is obedient to the will of the Supreme Soul and gives birth to the universe in consequence of His close association with it. Hence *prakriti* is looked upon as the wife of God and the Mother of the Universe. Both Vaishnavism and Saivism have recognised the appropriateness of this conception of the relation between God and Nature; and in Saivism we have *prakriti* and *Parama-purusha* even blended together in conception of the *Ardhanarisvara*—the God who is represented as half man and half woman. If we understand that Lakshmi represents in Vaishnavism the power of *prakriti*, we may easily make out the meaning and fitness of the function assgned to Her in Sri-Vaishnavism. Even according to the *Sankhya* of Kapila, *prakriti* is conceived to undergo all her modifications with a view to liberate all bound souls from their imprisonment in matter, and is for this reason compared to a kind and loving mother. In *Pauranika Sankhya*, Mother Nature happens thus to be the obedient and loving consort of Father God. Please note here that the feminine gender of the word *prakriti* in Sanskrit has not been without its influence in making Nature the kindly Mother of All, even as God is the great Father of All. Looked at in this light, what does the propitiation of Lakshmi really signify? It means this—that before we succeed in propitiating our God who is above and beyond Nature, it is necessary for us to propitiate Nature, if we are indeed anxious to get on well in life as well as after life. Those who want to live their lives happily and harmoniously for themselves and for others have to see that they do not foolishly violate the laws or oppose the irresistible forces of Nature. Hence the propitiation of the powers of Nature is always required in our own interest. Our ancestors of thousands of years ago achieved marked progress in religion by passing from Nature to Nature's God. In Ramanuja's *Visishtadvaita* philosophy, the oneness of the ultimate reality is not the result of any form of essential identity, but is based upon an organic union of the component entities making up the reality. Hence according to him the path of philosophic ascent is inevitably from Nature to Nature's God. And the function of mercy-seeking intercession in behalf of weak man, which is assigned in Sri-Vaishnavism to Lakshmi, the merciful Mother of All, enables us to see further that, in Ramanuja's view, the path of religious realisations also is in proceeding from Nature to Nature's God.

When philosophy taught our ancient sages how to anlyse the universe, and their constructive imagination led them to conceive the relation between God and Nature to be like that between a husband and his wife, it became perfectly natural for Vaishnavism to make Lakshmi the wife of Vishnu and the merciful Mother of the Universe. You know that the progress of religions takes place not unoften by the infusion of new ideas into old institutions. A great Arabic scholar writing about the religion of the Semites pointed out some years ago, with many examples, the tendency that there is in human societies to conceive their divinities almost unconsciously in the light of their own social organizations. If we have a community of people whose society is matriarchal in organisation, and among whom the mother is, therefore, the most prominent person in the family, their most natural conception of the deity happens to be as a goddess. They look upon the high supernatural being or beings at whose hands they seek sympathy and support as a mother. In other communities wherein the social organisation is patriarchal, where the father is the most authoritative figure in the family, the divine being is looked upon as a father. This state of affairs in human civilisation is indeed very well-known to students of anthropology. And we are able to make out with various kinds of evidence that the Dravidian people of South India possessed in the early days a matriarchal organisation of society, that among them the mother was accordingly the most important figure in the family, and that consequently the worship of the village goddess as *amman*—that is, as mother—came to be very prevalent among them. If we have a people among whom goddess-worship is prevalent, and if we want to introduce in their midst a newer and a higher religion, it turns out to be necessary to find a real place for a great goddess in that newer and higher religion. This was probably one of the reasons which led to the enthronement of Lakshmi in the religion of Ramanujacharya as the world's Merciful Mother, who is the ever-loving and ever-successful mediatrix between Her Lord God and the individual souls seeking the salvation of a perfected re-union with Him. Ramanuja's predecessors in the line of Sri-Vaishnava teachers had already given a prominent place to Lakshmi in their religion, probably because it happens to be a characteristic feature of Sri-Vaishnavism that it arose in the Tamil land and obtained its fresh nourishment largely from the inspired thoughts and sentiments of certain well-known Tamil poets and saints. The thought-influences proceeding from these poets and saints were taken up by Brahminical teachers, and were woven into the philosophy of Vaishnava Vedanta in a very remarkable manner. Such a mutual in-weaving of pious poetry and sublime philosophy is probably not seen in the literature of any other religion. The Sri-Vaishnavas often speak of their sacred literature as *Ubhaya-Vedanta*, that is, as a double Vedanta consisting of the Sanskrit philosophic Vedanta and the Tamil poetic Vedanta. And the association of Lakshmi or Sri with Vishnu as the intermediary between weak man and almighty God must also have been postulated in this manner in response to popular needs and influences; and it led to various consequences. Thus it is in all probability that Vaishnavism became here a religion in which Mother Lakshmi has to intercede for mercy between God and His children. And who are His children? All mankind—nay, all living beings.

If all mankind happen to be His children, and if Mother Lakshmi intercedes between weak and suffering mankind on the one hand and almighty God on the other, we can easily understand how in this religion none can be kept out of the Holy of Holies, and none can be looked upon as unworthy to receive the grace of God. If out of a family of a number of children, a mother keeps away any one child from sharing the kindly and merciful favour of the father, she certainly deserves to be characterised as an unnatural mother. Therefore in this religion there is an all-comprehensive divine graciousness which knows no exclusion. The reciprocity and the universality of divine and human love, as known to this religion, has in no small measure been the result of the Mother of All being made in it to intercede between God and all His children so as to temper His serene justice with tender mercy.

I have thus tried to indicate to you in a very brief outline the position occupied by Ramanujacharya in the development of Sri-Vaishnavism in our country. Vaishnavism, when adopted by Ramanuja, had already become Sri-Vaishnavism. In it the old Bhagavata doctrine of salvation through *bhakti* had been reasserted and developed beyond into the doctrine of *prapatti*. The decision to utilise the *Ubhaya-Vedanta* to Sanskrit philosophy and Tamil Vaishnava poetry as the basis of Sri-Vaishnavism had also been arrived at and practically carried out to a large extent by the predecessors of Ramanuja. Accordingly he was in no sense the pioneer of the popular religious movement out of which Sri-Vaishnavism arose in South India. He may be said to have come on the crest of the wave of this movement; and it received its final seal of authority and rational sanction at his hands. That he secured for it the full support of the Sanskrit Vedanta, and proved it to be a worthy means for the exaltation of the social virtues and the uplifting of the masses, is abundantly demonstrated by the events that filled his long life of courageous conviction and enduring sincerity and comprehensive humanity. Let me refer in illustration of this to the single instance of his having admitted the *paraiyas*—the *holeyas* as you call them here—as worshippers into the famous Vishnu temple at Melkote, which is, as you all know, situated within the Mysore State. The humanity and the courage involved in this noble act are both highly remarkable, and worthy of the enfranchising religious movement which attained its consummation through his work. After him others carried the stream of Vaishnava thought in various ways into various parts of this holy land of ours; and new forms of Vaishnava faith came into existence under new conditions. But these are matters which cannot be included within the scope of the persent lecture. The popularisation of the ideas of the Fatherhood of God, the Motherhood of Lakshmi, and the Brotherhood of Man in India is indeed in a notable degree due to Ramanuja and his work in life; and it is now a fact of history that to him may be traced more or less largely the beneficent religious influences that have proceeded from Ramananda, Kabir and Nanak. So far, Ramanuja's work in connection with the immemorial and ever progressive religious life of India has shown itself to be like the work of the prescient sower who sows good seeds in good soil : and we may therefore feel well assured that, under the quickening stimulation of the heavenly light of God-love, the harvest of the love of man to man as man will in due time be quite abundant and full of further hope and further promise in this our ancient and historic country, wherein he lived so well and laboured so nobly.

APPENDIX.

THE ALLEGED PERSECUTION OF THE JAINS BY VISHNUVARDHANA AND RAMANUJA.

BY

MR. S. KRISHNASWAMI AIYANGAR, M. A.

That it is impossible that either Vishnuvardhana or his successors could have sanctioned any such thing, is borne out by a number of incidents in their history. It was from the royal residence at Melkote that Vishnuvardhana makes a grant to the Saiva temple, at Chamundi Hill. He does receive the 'holy food' presented by the Jains after the consecration of the Jinalaya at Halebid and directs the God being named Vajaya Parsvanatha in honour of his victory. He honours Sripala Trividya Deva (the Jain controversialist) and even appoints him tutor to his children. It was about this time that the Vira Saiva (the so-called Lingayat) sect comes into prominence, so that in the course of the century Jainism was subjected to the simultaneous attacks of the Vaishnavas from the South and the Virasaivas from the North. The manner in which the Hoyasals—rulers and ministers alike—dealt with these rival sects is a supreme instance of their religious policy from which more modern rulers might learn lessons of wisdom. The minister of Vira Narasimha, by name Polalva Dandadhisa, founded the temple of Harihara, the image in which has the form combined of both Siva and Vishnu, thereby to indicate that there is actually no difference between the two. This achievement of a Vaishnava minister in reconciling the two opposing sects is a unique instance of a breadth of view in religion, which is hard to be found elsewhere at the time.

This was the feat of one of a class of persons, rulers and ministers, who had been devoted Vaishnavas. Vishnuvardhana after his conversion, perhaps through the course of his career, built temples dedicated to Narayana—at any rate endowed them richly,—such as Vira Narayana at Talakad, Vijaya Narayana at Belur, Kirti Narayana at Bannur, &c. In his progress through his dominions he had taken pains to enquire into the condition of these and other foundations, and saw that they were restored to their former position of eminence as places of worship. He did not in this show any partiality to one sect or the other. His general Gangaraja and his Jain wife Santala Devi, endowed Jain temples equally with his sanction as the several donations to Jain temples by this general and other Jain devotees would show. This example was followed by his successors, whether they were Vaishnava or Saiva, for some of them were of the latter persuasion also.

Thus then it is clear that in the matter of religion this Vaishnava Constantine Vishnuvardhana, as the disciples of Ramanuja took delight in calling him, was far from being a sectarian. No attempt was made at any uniformity of religious belief and the policy of the rulers was the most liberal that could be imagined.

THE

VAISHNAVITE REFORMERS OF INDIA

CRITICAL SKETCHES OF

THEIR LIVES AND WRITINGS

BY

T. RAJAGOPALA CHARIAR, M.A., B.L.

G. A. NATESAN & CO., SUNKURAMA CHETTI ST.,

Madras.

CONTENTS.

INTRODUCTION.

These are a series of Seven Essays on the Lives and Writings of the principal religious reformers of the Vaishnavite or Visishtadwaita School of India. The treatment is critical and historical; but special prominence has also been given to the literary side of this School's activity. A clear account of the growth of Vaishnavaism is intended to be conveyed by these Lives of Eminent Reformers, and reference has throughout been made to the development of doctrines. A special chapter is devoted to the exposition of the Visishtadwaita philosophy according to Ramanuja. The growth of Vaishnavaism in Northern India is briefly dealt with in the last Essay, that on Sri Chaitanya, wherein that great Saint's career is also fully described.

The Vedantic school of India consists of three main sub-divisions, whose founders, as popularly understood, are the great philosophers Sankaracharya, Ramanujacharya, and Madhwacharya. All these are Vedantists in the sense that they acknowledge the infallibility of the Upanishads, and follow its teachings, though differing in their interpretations of the same. All these three systems or at least the first two are of considerable antiquity. Sankara was preceded by ondapada, and he, by earlier teachers; and these again seem to have branched off from an earlier adwaitic school, which preached the one-ness of God, very possibly without the Maya-doctrine. The Ramanuja School, as we show in these pages, had an ancestry of great repute, commencing from the sage Bodhayana, who was perhaps only slightly removed from the author of the Vedanta Sutras, known as Badarayana and unanimously identified by Indian writers with Vyasa, the author of the Mahabharata. And if the Visishtadwaitic school in its practical and Sectarian aspect, is identical with the ancient *Bhagavata* School, and there is every reason to suppose, then indeed we shall be justified in saying that the origin of this school is to be fixed at some centuries prior to the Christian era. It is impossible to fix the exact dates of the Sutras, or the Bhagavadgita, or the earlier *Pancharatra Tantras* which are the foundation of the Bhagavata school; and any speculation as to their probable dates has not hitherto resulted in much positive good. But there are enough materials in existence from which the continuity of the Vaishnavite philosophy and traditions can be inferred; and the object of these pages is, in the main, to show the outline of the history of the Vaishnavite religious movement, as far as may be gathered from the literary works and traditions prevalent in the community.

Colebrooke, whose name is unmistakably connected with the origin of accurate knowledge in almost every department of Sanskrit scholarship, has left a clear if brief account of Ramanuja's Bhashya, and the Visishtadwatic School. Next to him Dr. Thibaut, whose labours in the field of Indian research, have earned for him the gratitude of all Hindus who value their philosophy, has made Ramanuja's Bhashya accessible to scholars by his monumental translation of the same. The Commentary on the Bhagavad-Gita, by Ramanujacharya, has been rendered into English by Mr. A. Govindacharya of Mysore, and is a useful book for reference. But with the exception of these works, the vast Vaishnavite literature, philosophical and religious, is yet inaccessible to the English-knowing public.

Some idea of its extent may be gathered from the references in these pages, wherein the most important works are named and their contents briefly described.

The Vaishnavite literature of South India has been deeply influenced by the Tamil works of the Alwars, of whom a brief account is to be found in the beginning of the last of the essays of this series. The Alwars were practically the earliest Brahmin missionaries to the South. They propagated the devotional aspect of the Vedanta in the Tamil land, and used the language of the people with great effect. The present work does not deal with their lives and writings, beyond making the brief reference already alluded to. But the Tamil poems of the Alwars will repay careful study by Tamil scholars interested in examining the history and progress of Vaishnavaism in India.

The teachers and reformers whose lives are described in these pages comprise, with one exception, the leading Vaishnava philosophers of South India, from the earliest time known to us. It will be seen that there is a continuity of the list from at least the beginning of the 9th century to the end of the fifteenth century. We have not cared to devote much space to questions of chronological nicety, for the simple reason that the traditional dates of these writers are in the main extremely probable and sufficiently accurate. In one instance, however, we have, at some length, discussed the date, namely the date of Sri Vedanta Desika's death; and this we have done, to explain an apparent discrepancy between the traditional date and the date disclosed by a Srirangam Inscription. As to the correctness of our conclusion on this point we leave it to specialists in Indian chronology to judge.

In the preparation of these pages, we have laid under contribution many existing works, literary and philosophical, in Sanskrit and Tamil, that have reference to Vaishnavaism. The Tamil *guruparamparas*, of which there are two or three recensions, are however the fullest biographies available and they have been fully utilized. Among works in English to which we are indebted, we must mention Mr. A. Govindacharya's numerous works on Vaishnavaism and especially his extensive Life of Ramanuja. Other works used by us are referred to in the course of these pages, and need no specific mention here.

The Life of Sri Chaitanya has been added here, as an example, and a remarkable example, of the product of Vaishnavaism in Northern India. It is not, however, clear that he owed anything directly to Ramanuja's teachings or the works of his School. But we have every reason to suppose, as we point out in the essay on Sri Chaitanya, that the Vaishnava Renaissance in Northern India was the result of Ramanuja's propagation of this faith in the South, and for this reason, we have traced the growth of Northern Vaishnavaism as an introduction to Chaitanya's Life.

In conclusion, we hope that in placing these pages before the public, we shall induce some at least who feel an interest in the development of Vaishnavaism, to examine the original materials and work out an ample history of which we have ventured to present the barest outline.

MADRAS:
1st *Feb.* 1909.

T. R.

Nathamuni.

DURING the latter half of the 9th century A.D. and the beginning of the 10th, there lived in the town of Srirangam, near Trichinopoly, a learned Vaishnavaite scholar named Ranganathacharya, more usually called Nathamuni, or the sage Natha. He is credited, in popular tradition, with having reached the fabulous age of over 500 years and to have closed his career at about 920 A. D. He was a native of Viranarayanapura, the modern Mannargudi, of the Chidambaram Taluk, in the dominions of the Chola rulers of the day, who had not yet risen to the greatness which preceded their final decline in the end of the 13th century. He was probably a descendant of early Vaishnava immigrants, from the banks of the Jumna and other parts of the north, who carried the Bhagavata or the Pancharatra cult to the south and laid the foundation for the spread of Vaishnavaism during the second to the seventh centuries of the Christian era which were the palmy days of the Pallava rule. The period just mentioned was the period of the Vaishnavaite Alwars, of whom the most revered is Satagopa or Nammalwar and the last is Tirumangaialwar. The latter was a contemporary of Tirugnana Sambandhar, the Saiva saint, and of the Pallava ruler Narasimhavarman I. of Kanchi (A. D. 625—645). The earlier

Alwar must have lived long before this period, possibly in the opening years of the Christian era. He was a native of the city of Kurukai, now Alwar-Tirunagari, near Tinnevelly, on the Tambraparani, in the kingdom of the Pandyas, and composed over a thousand stanzas in classical Tamil.

The literature of the Alwars presupposes a thorough knowledge of the Krishna stories and the stories of the earlier avatars of Vishnu, and the frequent impassioned references to such stories, even in the songs of the earliest of the Alwars, show that the South must have been flooded with these marvellous legends at a very early period. The story goes that Nathamuni while at the Vishnu temple of Mannargudi (Chidambaram Taluk), his native place, heard some Brahmins from the southern end of the Peninsula recite Tamil verses of Satakopa addressed to the Vishnu God of Kumbhakonam and was charmed with their sense and diction. He also found that these verses concluded with the words "These ten out of the thousand, composed by Satakopa." Nathamuni, thus placed in the track of research, seems to have finally recovered the whole of Satakopa's works, and he then arranged them and the extant works of the other Alwars into four collections of about a thousand stanzas each. He is also said to have brought about the system of regular recitation of these texts during the festivals of the God at Srirangam and the system obtains even to this day in most ancient temples dedicated to Vishnu. Nathamuni was, we may take it, well-versed in the Sanskrit literature of the day and is said to have been an adept in yoga and to have been the last to practise it in this part of India. He is said to have composed a work called *Nyayatatwa*, and a work on yoga philosophy, '*The Yoga Rahasya*.' Neither of the works seems to be extant now, but extracts from the former are given in the *Nyayasidhanjana*, a work of Venkatanatha, or the famous Vedanta Desika, a voluminous Vaishnava writer in Sanskrit and Tamil (A.D. 1269—1370), contemporary with the equally famous Vidyaranya, the Vijianagar minister. The Nyayatatwa seems to have been an elaborate treatise covering the whole field of philosophy from the point of view of the Ramanuja school and was developed further by later writers of the same school. Though possibly a good Tamil scholar, Nathamuni has left no Tamil work of his own behind, except a few memorial verses prefixed to the works of three of the Alwars, namely, Nammalwar, Vishnuchitta and Mathurakavi. Certain similar Sanskrit verses prefixed to the works of Nammalwar are also ascribed to him.

The ritual of worship as observed in Vishnu temples is based on two early standard works. One of them is known as the Vaikhanasa sutra, probably belonging to the black Yajur-Veda school. The other work is the Pancharatra Agama belonging to the extensive Tantra literature, popularly believed to have been composed by God Narayana Himself. In addition to laying down the modes of worship both in temples and at houses, the Agama contains rules of conduct for the Vaishnavaites and has a peculiar philosophy of its own, namely, that of the Bhagavata cult. The system is, of course, of very ancient date and is referred in the Mahabharata; and the Badarayana sutras on Uttara Mimamsa are understood to refer to this philosophy in the four sutras that conclude Pada II of the 2nd *Adhyaya*. Nathamuni's contribution to the ritual was the provision for the recitation of the Tamil vedas, as the works of the Alwars came to be collectively called, on appropriate occasions during the main festivals of the God. The immediate effect of such an arrangement was the critical study of the *Tiruvoymozhi* as Satagopa's work is usually called; and, from this time forward, a school of combined Sanskrit and Tamil scholarship arose, which developed into great importance in later days and finally divided the Vaishnava sect into the two forms of the Northern and the Southern or the Vadagalai and the Tengalai sections. The first commentary on the work of Sadagopa was, however, written only in the twelfth century towards the close of Ramanuja's life by a pupil of his. We have no means of ascertaining whether Nathamuni was a complete follower of all the doctrines that now go by the name of the Ramanuja school, but as he is traditionally considered the founder of that school, it is to be presumed that he was. We shall see further on that his grandson, Yamunacharya has really laid the foundation for all the doctrines that now go under Ramanuja's name. The doctrine peculiar to the Ramanuja school and considerably elaborated by the religious teachers who succeeded him is the doctrine of

Prapathi or surrender to God in absolute renunciation and faith. This doctrine is considered to have some slight basis in the Upanishads, but is not referred to in the Sri Bhasya of Ramanuja. It is practically founded on the Pancharatra Tantra referred to already and is a cardinal doctrine of the Vaishnavaite in his practical religion. It is, however, said to have been accepted and brought into practice by the sage Satakopa himself and by Nathamuni after him. The details of the doctrine are a fruitful source of controversy among the followers of Ramanuja and a very respectable amount of literature is even now extant on the subject.

A few anecdotes of Nathamuni's life are not uninteresting and may be mentioned. Readers of the Ramayana will remember how that great work is said to have been published for the first time by being sung in the court of Rama himself by two musical pupils of Valmiki, the author, who afterwards turned out to be Rama's sons. The Tamil songs of Satakopa are similarly sung to this day at Srirangam and other places and Nathamuni is said to have set them to music soon after his discovery of the work. The music was however, of a celestial kind not easily appreciable by ordinary folk. It is said that a dancing girl of the time sang songs in the celestial tune in the court of the Chola king of the day whose capital was Gangaikonda Cholapuram, in the Trichinopoly District, not far from the birthplace of Nathamuni. The king is said to have slighted the musician as he could not appreciate the celestial note and to have preferred another singer who sang the usual tunes. The former dancing girl soon after reached Viranarayanapura and sang before the god of that place and was warmly appreciated by Nathamuni as the music was after his own heart. The Chola king, on hearing of the Muni's appreciation, paid a visit to the shrine and meeting Nathamuni inquired the reason of his appreciation of the unfamiliar tune. It is said that Nathamuni directed a number of bronze cymbals of different weights to be sounded together and forthwith described correctly their different weights from a perception of the acute differences in the pitches of the notes. The king, admiring his peculiar powers, was satisfied of the superiority of the celestial tune to which the Tamil songs had been set. It may upset chronology, as ascertained at present, to be told that Gangaikonda Cholapuram was founded so early as the end of the 9th century, as it is usually associated with Rajaraja the Great, the Lord Paramount of Southern India who did not mount the throne till 985 A. D.; but we may take it that the site of the city was even then an alternative capital of the Cholas with Uraiyur, near Trichinopoly, which was no doubt the metropolis of the dominions. Contact with the Chola ruler is frequently mentioned both in the life of Nathamuni and of his grandson Yamunacharya and it is clear that the reference is to the Chola ruler when he went into residence at the secondary capital above referred to though no doubt both the sages spent a large portion of their later lives at Srirangam which was near the permanent capital Uraiyur. More correctly speaking,

Uraiyur had ceased to be the capital by this time. Tanjore had not yet become the capital of the Cholas.

Another anecdote in the life of Nathamuni connects him with the Tamil poet Kamban, the author of the Tamil Ramayana. It is said that this future Poet-Laureate of various kings composed his grand poem at the residence of his first patron Sadagopa Mudaliar at Tiruvannainallur, generally assumed to be the place of that name in the South Arcot District, and went about the country reading out portions of his work and soliciting favourable opinions of scholars. On reaching Srirangam he had to face an assembly of Pandits presided over by Nathamuni. It would seem that the latter was at first not appreciative but was finally won over by the intrinsic merit of the production. It is also supposed that an existing poem of over 100 stanzas on Satakopa is by Kamban and was composed to honour the Vaishnava Alwar. This anecdote may appear to be the invention of Tamil scholars of the Vaishnava persuasion to bring the eminent Kamban into the fold of the admirers of Satakopa and Nathamuni and is incompatible with the general opinion that Kamban was the court-poet of Kulottunga I. who reigned from 1070 A.D. But there is a tradition embodied in an ancient Tamil verse that Kamban composed his Ramayana in the Saka year 807, corresponding to A.D. 885. If this is to be relied upon as accurate, there is no inherent improbability in the story of young Kamban meeting the sage Nathamuni who must have been then well advanced in years.

In accordance with the custom of the times, Nathamuni went on a tour to Northern India, visiting the scenes of Krishna's birth at Muttra and the neighbouring places. His travels extended to the distant Badari or Badrinath on the north, Dwarka, Krishna's capital in Kathiawar on the west and Jagannath on the eastern coast. Nathamuni's travel was apparently for pilgrimage and not for religious propagandism, as was that of Sankara before him or of Ramanuja afterwards. It was in commemoration of this visit, with his son and daughter-in-law, to the banks of the Yamuna or Jumna that his grandson, born about A.D. 916, is said to have been named Yamuna. Nathamuni returned to the south in due course *via* Jagannath and is said to have lived a few years only after the birth of his grandson.

The story of Nathamuni's death is worthy of the ardent devotee that he is reputed to have been. One day a party of huntsmen headed by the Chola king rode past the residence of Nathamuni at Viranarayanapura. The sage, interrupted in his meditations by the attendant bustle, opened his eyes and, construing the party to be the divine Rama and his brother, on whom, we may suppose, his thoughts were wholly bent in meditation, followed the track of the party and walked with weary steps till the very gates of the Chola capital Gangaikondapuram, and there dropped down dead through sheer fatigue. His son Iswaramuni, the father of the famous Yamunacharya, duly discovered his whereabouts and did the funeral obsequies which the remains of the illustrious man demanded. The duration of Nathamuni's life must be left undetermined, as we cannot accept as reliable the traditional accounts which assign a period of from 350 to 500 years for the sage. We must, for the present, be satisfied with supposing that the sage was born somewhere in the first quarter of the nineth century and that he lived just over a hundred years, an age exceeded by Ramanuja himself, by Vidyaranya, and by his contemporary, Vedanta Desika, if the traditions that can be proved to have been current from the fifteenth century downwards be accepted as true.

Pundarikaksha.

NOTHING strikes us so peculiar in Hindu religious life as the high pedestal on which the spiritual teacher is placed and the implicit faith which the community has in him for weal or woe. Nor is the feeling one of recent growth. The Chandogya Upanishad says: "Only when studied under a teacher does any knowledge become excellent." Again "He who has a teacher alone knows." The Kathopanishad proclaims: "He who loves the Lord intensely and loves his Guru as the Lord Himself, is alone fit to receive the Highest Wisdom." And the Bhagavad Gita in Ch. XIII mentions the worship of the Acharya as an attitude worthy of attainment by the aspiring devotee. The puranic literature, as may be expected, amplifies these sentiments with exemplary stories of devotion and blind obedience on the part of the pupils. The story of Ekalavya in the Mahabharata is frequently referred to as to the efficacy of Guru-worship even when the Guru himself is indifferent. For this Ekalavya, who was refused instruction by Dronacharya, the famous teacher of the Pandus and Kurus, set up an image of Drona and, by ardent practice in the inspiring presence of that image, attained to such eminence in the use of the bow and arrow that Drona himself was staggered, and rather cruelly demanded the surrender of his thumb, which order the pupil duteously obeyed. It is therefore, a characteristic feature of the Hindu pupil that he is brought up under a system which places the personal influence and inspiration of the teacher as a more potent factor in effective instruction than all the industry and the intelligence of the pupil himself. And great teachers, geniuses though some of them have been, have studiously refrained from asserting any doctrine as of their own invention and have always modestly and gratefully referred to their Guru as the origin of all their power and the source of their inspirations. The word 'Upanishad' has been interpreted to mean 'Secret doctrine' or '*Rahasya*' and the greatest caution is observed before a teacher will freely impart it to a pupil. It appears to us moderns a mistaken policy to restrict the spread of knowledge of whatever kind, and the spirit of secrecy or disinclination to teach the greatest truths seems more worthy of the inventor of a new manufacturing process, jealous of the infringement of his rights and desirous of turning his knowledge to the best pecuniary advantage. The explanation seems to be, in part at least, that in times when manuscripts were rare or possibly writing was unknown, all knowledge was confined in the memory of a few learned men and the system continued long after the need for it ceased. But there was another factor in question which certainly helped to perpetuate the system of secret instruction. That was the necessity felt by the teacher to ascertain the fabric of the pupil's mind and ensure its being of a sufficiently close texture for the purpose both of retaining what is imparted by him and of afterwards utilizing it for the pupil's further spiritual advancement. It is not a proposition difficult to maintain that certain positions in philosophy appear untenable to minds constituted in one way but are lucidly self-evident to other minds that have had a different course of preparatory training. This is to some extent true of the material sciences as well: but these latter are more dependent on the conclusions of observation and experiment in the external world than the science of the soul and its relationship to the cosmos and the universal Self. Hence in spiritual matters all teachers of the world have insisted upon the necessity of a certain reserve in imparting serious instruction to pupils who are only yet feeling their way or possibly are adversely inclined. In the view of those teachers (and they are a majority) who hold that realisation of the Self is the ultimate goal of man and has to be learned by constant practice in seclusion and with the senses under control, the presence and active advice of one who has experience in the process are absolutely necessary. It is, therefore, not strange that for ages India has held the spiritual Guru to be indispensable and "*Acharya-devo bhava*" the motto of every student under spiritual instruction.

We have been led to make these reflections for the purpose of explaining the system of maintaining succession lists of teachers among the followers of every sect of Hinduism and more especially the Ramanuja school. The head of this list is Saint Satagopa, the author of the Thousand Tamil Songs, referred to already and the next name is that of Nathamuni himself, of whose life a brief sketch has been given already in these pages. In spite of the long interval of time between these two sages, the fact of the one being named as the other's successor is explained by the statement made by the followers of this school that Nathamuni saw the saint in Yogic vision and was directly instructed by him. We may, however, take it that for historical purposes the founder of both the theoretical and practical aspects of the Visistadwaita school in its outline is Nathamuni himself and that this great teacher had a respectable following of pupils imbued with his views and of sufficient learning to maintain them in controversy. Sage Nathamuni is said to have had eight pupils, of whom Pundarikaksha was the most important and is recognised as having continued the spiritual teachings of his preceptor. He is said to have been born about A. D. 826 at Tiruvallari, North of Srirangam, in the Choliah caste of Brahmins. It is said of Pundarikaksha that on one occasion he was deputed by Sage Nathamuni to escort his wife Aravindappavai to the residence of her father Vangip-purathachi as he was called. While there, Pundarikaksha who was of inferior caste was served with stale food, regardless of his being an honoured guest from the residence of Nathamuni. The latter on hearing of this fact and that the pupil himself never resented the apparent indignity but accepted it cheerfully as a favour, was greatly pleased with Pundarika's indifference to honour, and, noting it as a mark of high spiritual advancement, called him by the name of "Uyyakkondar" or "Saviour of the new Dispensation," a name by which he is now usually known. We had occasion to mention on a previous page that Sage Nathamuni made a visit to the banks of Jumna in the North and had a son, born to Isvara Muni, his son, named Yamunacharya after the God of that place. We are assured that Nathamuni foresaw the birth of the child some years before e event and commissioned his pupil Pundarikaksha to be spiritual guardian of the boy and instruct him in the ways of the new faith. Nathamuni, in his later life, was frequently subject to spiritual trance, an ecstatic state known as *Samadhi* when the subject sees nothing but God and is practically lost to the external world. Nathamuni was, we are told, in this *Samadhi* state for long periods at a time before his final end and in consequence had entrusted to Pundarikaksha the duty of instructing his grandson whose arrival he had fondly been watching. Pundarikaksha in his turn commissioned his senior pupil Ramamisra, native of Manakkal, also near Srirangam, to perform the office of Guru to the long-expected grandson. Ramamisra is the next in spiritual succession after Pundarikaksha and is chiefly remembered as the spiritual instructor of the great Yamunacharya, of whom we shall have more hereafter. Neither Pundarikaksha nor Ramamisra is known to have left any literary work behind them. We may suppose that their time was chiefly taken up with teaching and consolidating the doctrines of the New School of Sri Vaishnavas which had their origin with Sage Nathamuni as we have seen already. The saintly and exemplary lives of these men and their adoption of the Pancharatra cult must have contributed to their being respected by the community in general and followed by an ever-increasing group of ardent followers. A new religious creed usually courts strong opposition by adopting an aggressive attitude, but the early Vaishnavas of whom we are writing seem to have been very mild and non-aggressive in their ways and to have been treated by the surrounding community with kindliness and respect.

The truth is that both the Adwaita and the Visistadwaita Schools were the simultaneous expressions of a natural reaction from the sacrifice-ridden *Purva Mimamsa* schools of Guru and Kumarila, which held the field in philosophical speculation during the centuries immediately preceding the times of Sankara, and were in their turn the outcome of the disgust at the development of philosophical Buddhism and its levelling and atheistic tendencies. The Vaishnava School, instead of starting with a daring new philosophy, collected the forces of conservatism by accentuating a life of purity and high morality, and gave the death-blow to sacrificialism which had out-grown its original purpose and begun to deny God; while the Monism of Sankara won the sympathy of the intellectual among the community by its all-embracing subtlety and covert denunciation of mere Karma and Vedic ceremonial under the guise of the doctrine of illusion. It is difficult historically to say whether the subordinate place assigned to Karma-kanda in the two new phases of Hinduism was the result of an unconscious adjustment to the state of things that had resulted from the sustained attack of Buddhism on the sacrificial system generally, or, whether the original founders of these systems perceived the philosophical absurdity of inculcating the worship of various powers of the Earth and the Heavens simultaneously with the doctrine of Unity of God which was the corner-stone of each of the systems. Whatever the reason may be, the fact is clear that sacrificial observances were relegated to an inferior place in both these systems, though not boldly rejected as injurious or degrading. To the school of Sankara, the performance of ritualistic karma is a hindrance to true spiritual progress. It may be tolerated till the true vision of unity arises, but is afterwards of no further use. The Visistadwaitic School disapproves of all karma which is done for worldly or transient results and considers that the best antidote to its evil effects is the renunciation of all attachment to the fruits thereof. While theoretically therefore the Karma Kanda is valid and binding in the view of both systems, the practical effect is, as indicated above, that it stands neglected by Vedantins throughout except for purposes of deriving exegetical rules for application in the later Mimamsa.

It is for this purpose rather than as a help to the performance of sacrifices that the *Purva Mimamsa* has been studied in the ages after Sankara.

The study has been a matter of mere academic interest and the maxims evolved from the various sections of the old Sutras were applied to the interpretation of the Upanishads and of the Smrithis, sometimes relevantly, sometimes as the fancy of the author suggested. The latest and the best exposition of the subject, in the *Bhatta Dipika* of Khandaḍeva, of about the eighteenth century A. D., learned as it is by the profuse admixture of the terminology of modern Sanskrit logic, makes no attempt to explain the *modus* of the rituals, but, taking it always for granted, discusses the *ratio-decidendi*, so to speak, of each topic with a subtlety, and power of expression which only those trained in the logic school can appreciate. We mention these matters to show that neither the fact of the continuous study of the Mimamsa in later times nor the performance of occasional sacrifices by Brahmins under the patronage of petty rulers of various States, need blind us to the fact that the sacrificial system lost its real hold on Brahminic India several centuries back, and that the main cause was the effect of covert antagonism towards that system of both the Sankara and the Ramanuja schools.

The special influence of Vaishnavaism on the South Indian people, an influence which had its origin in the times now discussed, and has continued its action down to the present day, is of a two-fold character. In the first place, it loosened the hold of its followers on the various minor gods and goddesses who were generally propitiated with a view to the attainment of various worldly objects. An early Smrithi work like the voluminous digest of Hemadri, or *the Madhaviya*, shows the vast number of puranic ceremonies, *vratas*, fasts and feasts which were observed by the Hindus generally in honour of various deities like the sun, the moon, the planets, etc., on almost every imaginable day on which a particular *Tithi* or *Nakshatra* or a stellar or lunar conjunction happened to fall. Some of these ceremonies were considered *Nitya* or compulsory and some were *Kamya* or optional. But it became the fashion to resort to them largely and no doubt the main motive-power in keeping up the system was the full employment it furnished, and the remuneration it offered, to the Brahmin class, especially when the sacrifices fell into comparative disuse. Now Vaishnavaism checked this elaborate ceremonial by interdicting its votaries from the worship of any deities except the highest known to it, who was the God Narayana of the Upanishads, the primal cause of all things. The stringent, if somewhat illiberal observance of the Sri Vaishnavites in not recognising, as objects of worship, deities other than Narayana, had its origin in the desire to carry to its logical conclusion the principle of the Unity of the godhead and the undesirability of praying for any worldly benefits in the presence of the deity. The cosmopolitanism of the Adwaitin to whom one personal God was as good as another and both were simply of 'phenomenal' importance, it is not open to the Vaishanvite to adopt. Though the exclusiveness of the

Vaishnavite in the choice of a name to his one Deity is apparently of questionable merit at the present day and has sufficed to dub him as sectarian and bigoted, his attempt to free Hinduism of all but the purest form of worship of a single Deity deserves to be appreciated. Dr. Thibaut has pointed out that there is nothing sectarian in the philosophy of the Ramanuja school. In practical religion, devotion to one Deity was the teaching of this school, and the object was to elevate Hinduism to its pristine purity before non-Aryan influences had played upon it and instilled into it Tantric ritual and diversity of divinity.

Again, the rapid conversion to Vaishnavaism of large numbers of the masses of the people who were beyond the influence of Brahminism and mere philosophy, is another notable feature of this school, the germs of which we perceive even in the earliest times. While the Vedic Hindu strove to brand the non-Aryans as 'Dasyus' or 'thieves' and kept them at a distance, early Brahminism improved upon the treatment by making a monopoly of religious instruction and keeping Sudras and the lower orders generally outside its pale. In fact both the Mimamsas have constructed what they call the "*apa-sudra-adhikarana*" wherein they demonstrate that none but those of the three higher castes are entitled to recite the Vedas or undertake the study of the Upanishads. The Smrithis have further prescribed choice punishments for the Sudra who breaks the rule or even listens to a Vedic text when being chanted. In the face of this strict monopoly, it is to the credit of Vaishnavaism that it has been able to bring the lower classes into its fold and extend to them the privilege of knowing God and of attaining liberation. The agencies employed by Vaishnavaism in effecting this silent revolution were two in number, referred to already in a different connection in the life of Nathamuni. One of them was the doctrine of *prapatti* or surrender to God, which was conceived as demanding no caste status or educational qualification. The other was the adoption for religious purposes of the works of the Alwars and making them the common property of all classes, Brahmins and non-Brahmins alike. The former of these matters will receive some detailed notice on a future occasion and need only be referred to slightly at this stage.

We shall find in the succeeding articles that these special features of Vaishnavaism, namely, the tacit discarding of Vedic sacrificial ritual, the worship of a single deity, and the adaptation of the religion to the needs of non-Brahmins—features which have been described in some detail once for all now, as they have been present at the very beginning—were constantly kept in mind by each succeeding generation of teachers and contributed largely to the popularity and rapid spread of this form of Hinduism.

Yamunacharya.

THE chief incidents in the life of Yamunacharya are narrated in the existing works on the lives of these teachers with an amount of unanimity which goes far to show that what we now know about him is fairly accurate and reliable. He was born in the city of Viranarayanapura, the modern Mannargudi, in the South Arcot District, a few years after the beginning of the 10th century A.D. As the grandson of the great Nathamuni, he was doubtless well-cared for and properly educated in the Sanskrit lore of the day. It was Ramamisra, the pupil of Pundarikaksha, who helped the father Iswara Bhatta to initiate the boy Yamuna in the study of the Vedas, after he was duly invested with the sacred thread at about the age of eight. His intelligence and retentive memory soon attracted attention and placed him at the head of his schoolmates. We are told that the precocious boy would often slip away from school, and, when chid about his truancy, would reply that he had nothing new to learn for the day, but that his fellow pupils were simply going over what he had already learnt.

The teacher of Yamuna was a scholar who gloried in the expressive title of Mahabhashya Bhatta or Doctor of Grammar. The doctor, albeit his learning, was but a poor pundit and had to submit himself to one Akki Alwan, the Court Pundit of the Chola King at his capital Gangai Kondapuram. Akki Alwan, basking in the sunshine of royal favour, lorded it over all the pundits of the day, and our Bhatta among the rest, by exacting a yearly tribute from them. The collector of the tribute, on one occasion, reached Yamuna's school when his teacher was away and explained the purpose of his call. In a spirit of bravado Yamuna replied that no tribute would be given and that Alwan might be so informed. The angry reply came in due course that Alwan would not tolerate the impertinence, and that the unruly pundit must stand a contest of disputation with him or submit at once. Yamuna quieted his trembling teacher who was all for submission to the cruel Court Pundit, and sent a spirited verse* in reply intimating that he was capable of holding his own and beating down the enemy in any shashtraic disputation. We are next told, that the king at the instigation of his sagacious consort, who foresaw, not without some relish, trouble for the unpopular Alwan, sent the state palanquin and a bodyguard to escort the bold scholar who was to beard the lion in his den.

Yamuna, now a hero to the village, came with a large group of friends, who proclaimed in the manner usual in Oriental Courts, the learning of Yamuna and his matchlessness in Mimamsa and Vedanta scholarship.

---

* न वयं कवयस्तु केवलं न वयं केवलतन्त्रपारगाः ।
अपितु प्रतिवादिवारणप्रकटाटोपविपाटनक्षमाः ॥

A romantic touch is given to the succeeding incidents by our being told that the royal pair watched Yamuna entering the palace, and the queen, prepossessed by the young and, no doubt, attractive face of the Brahmin scholar, went so far as to claim a victory for him in the approaching contest. The king, piqued into supporting his Pundit, staked half his kingdom, we are told, on the event. Yamuna was duly escorted to the royal presence and took the place assigned to him. A Vedantic disputation then commenced in which, we are told, Yamuna gained a complete victory and Akki Alwan had to accept the public defeat.

The story of Yamuna's victory will not be complete without our adding that Yamuna is said to have propounded three puzzles to Akki Alwan at his own request, and that Akki Alwan in dismay, was powerless to answer them. These puzzles were in the form of statements of which Akki Alwan undertook to establish the negative by his arguments. They were: Our king is all supreme; the queen is chaste; your mother has issue. It is easily seen that to admit the propositions implied in the negatives of the first and second of the above, would have been highly ungrateful and imprudent in the Court Pundit, while the absurdity of the negative of the third is patent to all. We shall not waste our time in expounding Yamuna's supposed answers in support of these rather silly statements. It is only proper to add that the incident of the puzzles is omitted in some accounts of Yamuna's life and may be a later addition intended to give zest to the story of the victory. It is more to the purpose to state that the gracious Chola queen in great pleasure hailed Yamuna as '*Alavandar*' in Tamil, meaning 'the victor,' a name by which Yamunacharya has been best known ever since, and that the king, true to his promise, granted him a portion of his territories to rule and enjoy.

The remainder of Yamuna's life is divisible into two portions, the respective durations of which we have no means of ascertaining. During the first portion, he was in enjoyment of the lands granted by the king and lived a life of pleasure and luxury. He had married and had four sons. He lived in a palace and had a large retinue. He forgot the higher life lived by his grandsire Nathamuni, and the latter's poor followers and pupils could not gain access to the presence of the lordly Alavandar. At last, the awakening came. Ramamisra, the pupil of Pundarikaksha, succeeded, after great efforts, in gaining an interview with Yamuna, and intimated that he was in charge of a valuable treasure of Nathamuni, in trust for Yamuna. Yamuna agreeing to receive it, the two went together to the shrine of Srirangam, where Yamuna was led to the presence of the Deity by Ramamisra and made to accept Him as the treasure that Nathamuni had left for his grandson. Yamuna, whose eyes were now fully opened to the evils of the unprofitable life that he had hitherto led, accepted the duty of love to God in all humility, and, throwing up his life of a householder, assumed the garb of a Sanyasin, pledged to a wholly spiritual life.

He took up his residence at Srirangam and led a life of absolute renunciation, composing philosophical works and expounding the doctrines of the Visistadvaitic school. Srirangam became a stronghold of Vaishnavaism. Worship at the temple and participation in the regular services both in and out of the temple precincts furnished occupation for a large number of the ardent devotees, while the lectures of Alavandar and the frequent discussions held in his presence gave great impetus to Sanskrit study in general and that of the Upanishads and the Sutras in particular. The Upanishads, the Gita, and the Vedanta Sutras, had long before this established their claim to pre-eminence in Hindu philosophy and had been styled 'the three *Prasthanas*' or primary works on philosophy. Every offshoot of Hinduism from the time of Sankara downwards based its main doctrines on its own interpretations of these three important works; and the pioneers of Visistadvaitism naturally turned their energies towards the task of textual interpretation of the same three works. In Yamuna's time, the work of oral interpretation was proceeded with, while the formal composition of text-books on the subject was reserved for the next generation under the guidance of Sri Ramanuja.

It is well to bear in mind in this connection that the Visistadvaita school claims a venerable ancestry for its origin, commencing almost from the times of the author of the Sutras, Vyasa or Badarayana. A sage Bodhayana composed a *Vritti* or extensive commentary on the Sutras. The doctrines of the Vritti are understood to be refuted in many places in the existing commentary of Sankaracharya, although, following a well-understood literary etiquette, the actual author Bodhayana is not quoted by name. A gloss on the Vritti is known to have been composed by Acharya Tanka who is quoted frequently in the works of Ramanuja under the style of *Vakyakara* or glossator. Dramidacharya, a scholar of the Tamil land as his name implies, then wrote a fuller exposition of the Sutras and this came to be called the Bhashya. The references to the Bhashya in Ramanuja's works are to this commentary. One *Srivatsanka* is also mentioned as the author of a commentary on the Dramida Bhashya. He seems to have been also a very ancient writer as he is styled 'Bhagavan,' a term of great reverence. Another writer Guhadeva by name, also wrote a work on the Visistadvaita philosophy. But all that we possess of these works from that of Bodhayana to that of Guhadeva are the names of the authors and a few short extracts from the Vritti and the Bhashya in Ramanuja's works. However, there is no doubt that in Yamuna's time there was an extensive literature of the Visistadvaitic school continuing the traditional interpretation of Bodhayana and diverging in important points from that of the Sankara school. Yamanucharya himself refers, in his *Sidhi Traya* to be presently mentioned, to a series of authors of both the schools who preceded him and composed works explanatory of the Sutras. They are the Bhashyakrit (apparently Dramidacharya) Srivatsankamisra, Tanka, Bhartriprapancha Bhartrimitra, Bhartrihari, Brahmadatta, Sankara, and Bhaskara. The first three names belong to the Visistadvaitic, and the rest apparently to the Sankara or allied schools. The Dramidabhashyakara, whose name is otherwise unknown, preceded Sankara and wrote a rather concise commentary on the Sutras. He seems also to have commented on the Upanishads, and this commentary seems to have been an extensive work, so says Anandagiri, the well-known commentator of Sankara's works, in the opening lines of his gloss to Sankara's Chandogya Commentary.

We may mention also that the *Vedartha Sanaraha* of Sri Ramanuja helps us somewhat to supplement the information on ancient writers given by Yamunacharya. Ramanuja mentions a list of over seven authors, namely, Bodhayana, Tanka, Dramida, Guhadeva, Kapardi, Bharuchi, etc., and the commentator Sudarsana Bhatta explains that Tanka was also known as Brahmanandin, a fact vouchsafed for by Vedantadesika also in his commentary *Tatwatika* on the Sri Bhashya. There is no doubt that Tanka is the Vakyakara referred to in later works, and that he preceded Dramida in the exposition of the Sutras. The fact that Dramidacharya wrote an extensive bhashya on the Upanishads from the standpoint of Visistadvaita also shows that Sankara was not the pioneer in this kind of work, a fact admitted by Sankara himself, and also explains why Ramanuja and others of his school before him did not set about a regular commentary of the

Upanishads. Dramida's work has, however, been entirely lost and the only convenient and full commentary on the Upanishads possessed by the Visistadvaitic school is that of the learned Rangaramanuja Muni, a writer of comparatively recent date, not to be confounded with the great Ramanujacharya.

The *Sidhi Traya,* of which mention has been made already, is the first and most important of the works of Yamunacharya. It contains 3 sections called the *Atma-Sidhi,* the *Iswara-Sidhi,* and the *Samvid-Sidhi* and is intended to establish the real existence of the individual and supreme souls and refute the doctrine of Avidya. It is written in a stiff prose style mixed with terse *anushtubh Karikas* in the manner of early philosophical works of which the *Tantra Vartika* of Kumarila Bhatta furnishes a good example. The last section is entirely in verse and is somewhat incomplete. As in the *Sloka Vartika,* (as the first part of Kumarila's work is called) the language is spirited and frequently graceful. In one place our author says, in declining to accept a mere assertion of the opponent, "All this dogmatism may carry weight with (blind) believers; we are non-believers (in your doctrines) and require logic to convince us."* A most rational position this, which every school of Hindu thought, not excluding the author's will do well always

---

* हन्त ब्रह्मोपदेशोऽयं श्रद्दधानेषु शोभते ।
वयमश्रद्दधानास्स्मो ये युक्तिं प्रथियामहे ॥

88 Sidhi Traya, Benares Ed.

to bear in mind. In refuting the absolute-indentity doctrine derived by Sankara from the Upanishad text '*Ekamevadvitiyam*,' our author makes a statement of some historic interest. He says, "To say that the Chola king *now reigning* in this country, is *all* supreme and without a second, can only exclude the existence of another monarch equal (in power) to him; it cannot imply the denial of the existence of a wife, sons or servants of such a monarch."* Though the king is not mentioned by name, we may probably identify him with the Chola King Rajaraja the Great A.D. 985—1012), the undoubted Lord Paramount of India at the time, who fully deserved the epithet '*Samrat*' or 'Emperor' here bestowed on him, as he conquered the Vengi kingdom, Orissa, and Ceylon, defeated the Rashtrakutas, and was the most powerful of the whole of the Chola dynasty. It is interesting to observe from the list of commentators given above that the great Bhaskara, mentioned after Sankara and known as the founder of the Bhedabheda Vada, preceded our author. A reference to '*Souresam Vachas*' in the Atma-Sidhi also shows that our author was well-acquainted with the able commentary on the Sankara Bhashya by Sureswaracharya, the pupil of Sankara. We have been able to trace no explicit reference either to Goudapada, the predecessor of Sankara, or even to the Nyayatatwa of

* यथा चोलनृपः सम्राडद्वितीयोऽस्ति भूतले ।
इति तत्तुल्यनृपतिनिवारणपरं वचः ॥
न तु तत्पुत्रतत्भृत्यकलत्रादिनिवारणम् ॥

Nathamuni, which latter work, of course, our author must have known well. We shall in this connection content ourselves with giving one specimen of the subject-matter of Sidhitraya, which will at the same time furnish a sample of the style of the author in philosophy metrically treated. Says Yamunacharya*: "The 'Individual Soul' is a separate entity in each body, which is by nature, eternal, subtle, and blissful. It is distinct from the body, the senses, the mind, the vital air, and the intellect, and is self-contained." The Sidhitraya is quoted frequently by Ramanuja and no doubt was largely the basis of his able refutations of Sankara's views in the Sri Bhashya.

The next work of Yamunacharya that we shall notice is the *Agamapramanya*, a work the object of which is to establish the orthodoxy of the Bhagavata or Pancharatra school. Mention is made of a *Kashmira-Agmapramanya* of the same author at the end of the former work; but the work is lost now and nothing is known about it except that it sought to establish the genuineness of the *Ekayana Sakha*, the fundamental text of the Bhagavata school, as a branch of the Veda. The Agamapramanya, is, like the Sidhitraya, in prose and verse, the verse being generally in Anushtubh metre and used only when a sententious *resume* or pointed exposition is deemed necessary. We had occasion to refer to the Pancharatra school more than once

---

* देहेन्द्रियमनःप्राणधीभ्योऽन्योऽनन्यसाधनः ।
नित्यो व्यापी प्रतिक्षेत्रमात्मा भिन्नः स्वतः सुखी ॥

before, and we shall use the present context to make some observations in detail about that school. It is well-known that the various Vedas were studied in different *Sakhas* or recensions. One of these was the Ekayana Sakha probably of the White Yajur Veda. The various Sakhas had different ritual books, dealing with the domestic rites of his followers; the Apasthamba of the Black Yajur Veda may be mentioned as an illustration. It is an article of absolute faith among the twice-born of India that every person should stick to his Sakha and perform only the ceremonials prescribed in it. The *Ekayanins* had several such special rites. One peculiarity in their daily life may be mentioned. The Ekayanin, who, in austerity of life, was almost a monk, but without the restriction of celibacy divided the day into five periods. First came the period of *Abhigamana* or approaching God, which the Ekayanin did as soon as his daily ablutions and *Japas* were over. The next period, from about half-past eight to midday, was allowed to be devoted to wordly life, the earning of one's livelihood by irreproachable means, etc. This was called the *Upadana* period. The next period was styled *Ijya*, literally, *sacrifice*. The Ekayanin cared not for the Vedic sacrifices. His sacrifice was the *Pancha-yagna* ending with the midday prayer to God, the placing before Him of all that he had prepared of food etc., and included his meal-taking, which was considered an act of religious nature. The next period was that of *Swadhyaya* or study, which each householder regulated as suited his taste or capacity. The last period of the day of 24 hours thus divided was called *Yoga* or quiet contemplation, when thoughts of the Almighty engaged the devotee before he went to bed. This simple-living Ekayana sect of almost prehistoric times seems to have grown into the Bhagavata sect even before the period of the Mahabharata and to have developed for itself a large sectarian literature which came to be known as the Pancharatra Tantra. The Tantra literature of India with its divisions of the Pancharatra, the Boudha, the Saiva or the Pasupata, and the Sakta branches, is so very extensive that it would fill a library by itself. It is not proposed to describe this, even if it were possible to do so. It is enough to say that the Pancharatra appears to have been one of the earliest of these and was so called because it was supposed to have been promulgated during five nights by God Narayana himself. It is now only partially extant and a small portion only again is available in print in Telugu character. The Tantra is divided into various *Samhitas* which bear the names of various sages or ancient writers. The most important of them are the *Satwata*, the *Poushkara* and the *Jayakhya* samhitas. These are described as *Divya* or uttered and promulgated by God Narayana directly. The others were promulgated through various sages, whose names, as in the case of Smriti writers, is legion. In one work alone, the *Pancharatraraksha* of Vedanta Desika, as many as thirty of these are named; and many of them must have been long, judging from the numbers of the chapters quoted. The chief topics discussed are the modes of service in temples, the details of a Srivaishnava's or Bhagavata's life, and the most suitable general method of salvation, namely, *prapatti*, mentioned already in these pages. It speaks much both for the antiquity of the sect and its literary activity that the works are collectively mentioned in the Mahabharata and some of the ancient puranas, with approval and not in condemnation. The large number of non-Brahmin conversions made by the followers of this sect later on must have reacted on the Brahmin portion of it, and practices unusual among the Brahmins of the day must have crept in, which brought some disrepute on the sect as a whole. This explains why Sankaracharya in his commentary on the four Sutras II. 2. 42 to 45 treats them as intended to refute the orthodoxy of the sect in matters wherein it differs from the rest of the Brahmin class. The Bhagavata, unlike the various heretical philosophers whose views are already criticised in the second pada, admittedly upholds Brahman or Vasudeva as alike the material and the instrumental cause, like the Vedantin. Why then is he being refuted? Sankara explains, "On this point he is all right, but there are some tenets of his which are *unvedic* and so Badarayana refutes him." What Badarayana exactly meant to state in the four Sutras referred to is not clear. According to Sankara they mean: "the Pancharatra is unacceptable (1) because it speaks of the creation of the soul as Sankarshana from Vasudeva, while the soul in the Vedanta is eternal; (2) because it inculcates the production of the mind from the *Jiva*, a thing equally unvedantic; (3) to suppose that the forms Sankarshana and the rest are identical with Vasudeva, would not mend matters, as the four-fold division would still be purposeless; and (4) lastly, the Tantra shows mutual contradictions in itself." This interpretation of the Sutras as the statement of four adverse arguments against the orthodoxy of the Pancharatra is elaborately opposed by Yamunacharya in the Agamapramanya, and the Visistadvaitic view is further set forth in the Sri Bashya. From these we gather that the four Sutras in the view of this school are not all adverse, but that the first two of them contain *prima facie* adverse arguments, while the last two refuse those arguments and maintain the orthodoxy of the Tantra. The last two Sutras would then stand thus:—" (3) But by taking the four forms, Vasudeva and the rest, as identical with Brahman, the objection, as to the soul's being born, is removed, (the purpose of the manifestations, like that of Avatars generally, being explainable always) and (4) the Tantra explicitly denies the fact of the souls having an origin." In other words it is said that the Pancharatra could hardly be discredited as containing points of erroneous philosophy which it has not, as practically admitted in the 3rd of the Sutras by Sankara himself. To confine ourself to the question of interpretation of the Sutras and not to dwell long on a subject which could hardly interest the general reader, one fact may be mentioned which goes far to show that the Visistadvaitic interpretation may in this, as in other cases, as pointed out by Dr. Thibaut, represent an earlier tradition which Sankara or his predecessors ignored. That is, the use of the particle तु in the middle of the Sutra 3 of the set is most usually indicative of a change of side in the argument, both in the *Purvamimamsa* and in the Vedanta. We can point out at least 5 other places in the Vedanta Sutras, especially in pada 3 of Adhyaya III, as instances of this use of the particle; and such instances of this use of the particle; and such instances are also so numerous in the Jaimini Sutras that the argument appears very convincing indeed. On the other hand, it has to be said in favour of the Sankara view that the Tantra must partake of the heretical nature of the other philosophies in whose company this is also found discussed. Against this, again, may be set Dr. Thibaut's opinion that 'it would not be unnatural to close the polemical pada with a defence of that doctrine which—in spite of objections—has to be viewed as the true one.'

The next work of Yamunacharya deserving mention is the summary of the Gita-teachings styled *Gitartha Sangraha*. No work of Yamunacharya shows so well as this does, how far Ramanuja was indebted to his predecessors in the elaboration of the Visistadvaitic system which he so completely carried out. In the *Sangraha*, Yamunacharya, in the course of about 30 verses in *anushtubh* metre, analyses fully the argument in the Bhagavadgita, as understood by the school represented by him. The Bhagavadgita is a work which, in spite of its great antiquity and sanctity, and apparent simplicity, has baffled many commentators and critics. To some, it appears full of contraditions; to others, it is a patchwork of three or four layers set one over another. To others again, the central theme is clear, while the work is full of digressions and repetitions. In this state of things it cannot but be important to know that as early as the 10th century, Yamuna, following antecedent oral teaching, analysed the work as a consistent exposition of the doctrine of Bhakti supplemented by a description of the Karma and Gnana Yogas as subordinate to the main doctrine. Unlike the case of the Vedanta Sutras, there is no internal indication here of the existence of any specific commentaries of the text, at the time of Yamuna's writing; but the probabilities are that Yamuna summarised the teachings handed down to him orally, rather than invented his system of interpretation. We have ample internal evidence in the *Gita Bhashya* of Ramanuja that he strictly conformed in his interpretations to the outline depicted in Yamuna's epitome. The general scheme of the Gita according to Yamunacharya my be described in a few words. We are told that the first six chapters of the 18 into which that work is divided, treat of Karma and Gnana Yogas, and close with a description of the Yoga state; the second batch of six chapters treat of Bhakti Yoga, while the last six deal with subsidiary topics which help towards the understanding of the rest, and conclude in verses 65 and 66 of Chapter XVIII with the enunciation of what is held to be the essence of all the secret teachings that have gone before. Yamuna, and following him, Ramanuja, work out the continuity of the thought in the whole work in a much more natural manner than is possible to infer from Sankara's explanations of the same poem. We cannot of course affirm that there are no forced constructions in Ramanuja's commentary; but we have found in many places where a different interpretation would suggest itself to us that Ramanuja adopted his construction specially to suit himself to the plan chalked out by Yamuna. We have in mind especially Chapters VIII and XII of the Gita. two short but extremely difficult chapters, where Yamuna's scheme of interpretation is closely adhered to, with a result that can hardly be called satisfactory from the point of view of the critical reader.

There is mention made of a work 'Mahapurusha Nirnaya' by Yamunacharya which is now lost to us; but of one other existing work we wish to make mention, on account of its high literary merit and the great hold it has on the mind of the religious Vaishnavaite. We refer to a devotional song or Stotra as it is called of about 75 stanzas, somewhat like the *Soundaryalahari* of Sankaracharya, but dedicated, as may be expected, to God Vishnu. The language is simple and chaste, the imagery is natural, and the sentiments are those of an earnest devotee who pours out his heart in the most direct language he can command. The work has been styled a '*Stotra-ratna*,' a gem of its class, and is explained by an ample commentary from the erudite scholar and philosopher, Vedanta Desika.* Having regard to this work of Yamuna, we may say of him that he combined in himself the characteristics of a poet and a philosopher, in a more real sense than we can do so of any other Sanskrit writer who claims such a distinction.

The personal life of Yamunacharya at Srirangam, where he mostly stayed after his spiritual conversion, was simple and without any stirring incidents. Religious persecution was never serious in India, and in the south, the Cholas, the chief reigning dynasty, were, at least at this time tolerant to the new faith, though they were of the Saivite persuasion. Yamuna was peacefully devoting himself to religious teaching and meditation. He once travelled as far as Trevandrum on the western coast to visit there the shrine of *Sri Padmanabha*, and returned home after the usual tour round the numerous Vishnu shrines in Travancore, Tinnevelly and Madura. It was by reason of this trip that Yamunacharya missed an engagement with one Kurukaikkavalappan, a pupil of the great Nathamuni, to whom the latter had entrusted the secret of Yoga or quick realisation of the vision of God. This holy man, requested by Yamuna to impart the great secret to himself, had fixed a particular date as that on which he would do so, that being also the time which the Yogi had, by his powers, ascertained to be the date of his death. Yamuna discovered when too late that he had missed the day assigned, and

* The text and commentary have been recently published at the Ananda Press, Madras, in Nagari characters.

thereby helped unconsciously, it is said, to make the secret of Yoga perish for ever with the said pupil of Nathamuni.

Another trip which Yamuna undertook, late in his life, was to Conjeeveram, whither he went, it is said to cast a look on the rising scholar Ramanuja, who, as yet a student, was early distinguishing himself and attracting the attention of all. Yamuna with the help of Kanchipurna, a Sudra pupil of his at Conjeeveram, who has since become canonised and has at present a special idol and shrine erected in his honour in the modern town of Small Conjeevaram, obtained a view of Ramanuja, but as the latter was in the company of his master Yadavaprakasa, an adwaitic teacher, he did not care to send for him or converse with him. After visiting the shrines at Kanchi and spending some time there, Yamuna duly returned to Srirangam. Yamunacharya lived to a good old age and died, it is said, at about 1040 A.D., having expressed with his last breath an earnest wish to see Ramanuja established at Srirangam as a staunch supporter and defender of the Vaishnavaite faith, a wish which Ramanuja was duly to fulfil in a most thorough manner. Yamunacharya left many* pupils behind him, some of whom had the privilege of instructing Ramanuja himself in various branches of study. The most important of such pupils were *Mahapurana*, *Goshtipurna*, *Sri Sailapurna* and

* As many as twenty are mentioned. See Mr. A. Govindacharya's Life of Ramanuja, p. 23. Sri Vedanta Desika gives a list of 15 in his *Rahasyatrayasara,*

Maladhara. Chotta Nambi and Pillai Arasu Nambi are named among his sons, but they are of no importance to the student of Vaishnavaism. We shall, therefore, address ourselves to the life and teachings of Ramanuja in the next article.

Ramanujacharya.

WE shall in this article describe briefly the chie events in the life of the great Ramanujacharya, the practical founder of the Visishtadwaita system, referring to the names and characteristics of the most important of his immediate followers, and shall conclude with a short summary of his philosophy as disclosed in his works.

We have seen that by the end of the tenth century A.D., Visishtadwaitism had greatly developed under Yamunacharya and had obtained a strong foothold in Srirangam with Conjeevaram, Tirupati, and a few other places, as rallying centres for the followers of this creed. Yamuna felt that among his immediate followers, there was no one who could exactly fill his place as the head of the New Dispensation. He, therefore, cast his longing eyes around among the younger men and surmised from personal observation and general report that the young Ramanuja, then a pupil under Yadavaprakasa, was, by intellect and character, the fittest person that could succeed him. He did not, however, wish to precipitate matters, but allowed them to take their own course, trusting that, under the guidance of Providence, all would end well.

Sri Sailapurna, already mentioned as a disciple of Yamunacharya, was established at Tirupati Hills, in service at the Temple of that place. He had two sisters, one of whom, Kantimati was married to one Kesava Somayaji of Sri Perumbudur about 10 miles from the Trivellore Railway Station, near Madras. This lady gave birth to Ramanuja, about the year 1017 A.D., and the uncle, Sir Sailapurna came down from the hills and was pleased at the benign and intelligent face of the child. He looked after the boy carefully and duly got him invested with the sacred thread at the proper age. After the usual preliminary studies in which Ramanuja, as may be expected, showed great capacity, a teacher, Yadavaprakasa by name, was selected for the higher course, and Ramanuja duly went to study with him. Here he was joined by a cousin of his, another nephew of Sri Saila, and the two, in the usual fashion of the day, boarded with the teacher and acquired proficiency in the secular sastras. When it came to the study of philosophy or the Upanishads, Ramauja found his master's explanations unsuited to his taste. He took objection to the interpretation of more than one passage, and suggested his own meanings, which hardly pleased the teacher. A coolness arose in consequence between master and pupil; we are told that the former, in combination with the other pupils, formed an unholy conspiracy to take Ramanuja on a long journey to Benares and get rid of him there. The unsuspecting Ramanuja accompanied the party; but while travelling in the jungles of the Vindhyan outskirts, his cousin Govinda Bhatta, into whose ears the news of the nefarious intention towards Ramanuja had oozed, appraised him of the impending danger and bade him escape somehow. Ramanuja, in sore straits, struck into a by-path and lost his way. The party proceeded without him and discovered, when too late, that he had slipped away. In great distress and much fatigued, Ramanuja wandered over the thickets, for a long time, unable to decide upon his course. He then met, as if by chance an old hunter and his wife, and of them he inquired the way. They said that they were going to the Satyavrata Kshetra, *i.e.* Conjeevaram, and bade him follow. The three travelled all the night. Towards dawn, the old man asked Ramanuja to fetch some water from a neighbouring well. When Ramanuja came back with the drink, the pair had mysteriously disappeared, and Ramanuja found to his wonder and delight that he had miraculously reached Kanchi itself, the tower of whose temple was visible to his eyes. He sped home, feeling sure that God in his mercy had come to his help. In due course the party of Yadava reached Conjeevaram after their travels and surprised to find Ramanuja, made up to him, as if nothing had happened. Ramanuja resumed his studies with Yadava, as before, but with some hesitation. The Adwaita interpretations displeased him more and more. It also happened that Yadava, called to exorcise an evil spirit that possessed the daughter of the King of the place, failed to quell it. The spirit, however, bowed to Ramanuja who accompanied Yadava, expressed its opinion of his greatness and departed in deference to his wishes. This incident embittered Yadava towards Ramanuja who had finally to give up his studies under such an uncongenial master. Ramanuja then attached himself to the service of the Devaraja Perumal at Kanchi where Kanchipurna, a non-Brahman disciple of Yamunacharya, was in daily attendance on he God. This devotee had the reputation of being in close touch with the God of his worship, who, it is said, assumed the ways of men towards the favourite and held discourse with him in human language.

Meanwhile Mahapurna, a disciple of Yamuna, who had been despatched by the Acharya and his followers to persuade Ramanuja to go to Srirangam and formally accept the new faith, reached Conjeevaram for the purpose, and with the help of Kanchipurna succeeded in his object. Ramanuja gladly agreed to pay his respects to the far-famed Yamuna and the two started towards Srirangam. They duly reached the northern bank of the Kaveri, when lo! a great concourse of Vaishnavas made their appearance in mourning procession, and Ramanuja ascertained, to his irreparable sorrow, that the great Yamuna had breathed his last and was being buried with holy honours on the banks of the Kaveri. Ramanuja hastened to have a last look at the body of the great guru and was surprised to see that three of the fingers of his right hand were closed in a deadly grip. He asked the bystanders if they were usually so. They replied that shortly before death, the veteran teacher had expressed three wishes and had closed his fingers in the act of counting them. The wishes were that a Visistadwaita bhashya should be composed on the Sutras of Vyasa, and that the names of Parasara, the author of the Vishnu Purana, and of St. Sadagopa should be perpetuated as a mark of gratitude to the two great men named. Deeply affected, Ramanuja proclaimed that, God willing, he would undertake the duties named and accomplish them speedily. No sooner was this statement made than the fingers opened out, we are told, of their own accord, and the assembled Vaishnavas herein read a sure sign of the coming greatness of the young man who stood before them. Ramanuja duly attended the obsequies of Yamunacharya but left Srirangam immediately after, and reaching Kanchi, resumed his duties there, in the company of the pious Kanchipurna.

Ramanuja was deeply impressed with the saintly character of this man and felt drawn towards him. Not caring for his inferior social status, he invited him for meals in his house and instructed his wife (for he had now married and had set up house-keeping for himself) to prepare food for him. The purna, after his temple services, went up to Ramanuja's house and being pressed for time, took his meals at once and departed, leaving word for Ramanuja who was away, that business called him back so suddenly. Ramanuja returned and saw his wife clearing the leaves on which the purna had taken his food, and washing generally the place and bathing herself to get rid of the impurity of the Sudra's contact. Ramanuja, who had, out of piety and respect, intended to wait upon Kanchipurna and eat after he had dined, (a thing unusual for a Brahman) felt greatly disappointed. He gently rebuked her for her illiberal spirit and felt that he was ill-matched in her.

Yamuna's death at Srirangam had left a void which his disciples were anxious to fill up; and old Mahapurna was again despatched to bring Ramanuja. As chance would have it, Ramanuja also thought of going up to Mahapurna for spiritual instruction, now that Yamuna was dead, and actually commenced his journey south. The two met at Madurantakam, and the impatient Ramanuja requested Mahapurna to instruct him in the mantra of the Vaishnavites immediately. Mahapurna complied, and the two proceeded to Kanchi, where Mahapurna (and his wife who had accompanied him) lodged in Ramanuja's residence. Ramanuja pursued his religious studies under the new guru and had a happy time of it. This was, however, marred by a petty quarrel which arose between the ladies, and Mahapurana, afraid that Ramanuja will take it too much to heart, if further ill-feelings arose, suddenly left Kanchi with his wife and proceeded to Srirangam. Ramanuja, who was away at the time of the incident, returned and finding from enquiry that his wife's pettiness was mostly to blame for the quarrel, felt sorely the affront to his master and feeling displeased with her altogether, sent her to her father's home finally, resolving to abandon the house-holder's life. He went to the presence of the God of Kanchi and there, with due ceremonies, donned the red robes of the Hindu Sanyasin, and thus broke all his family ties.

From the temple precincts of Kanchi, Ramanuja practised his austere Sanyasin's life and soon attracted followers. A native of Kuram, a neighbouring village was the first to be drawn to him. Kuresa, as he was called, was a wealthy and learned Brahman and became a life-long friend and follower of Ramanuja. Dasarathi. the sister's son of Ramanuja, was another who came to him and was one of his most beloved pupils ever after. Other persons sought him out, became his pupils and accepted his teachings. Yadavaprakasa, his old teacher, was, we are told, persuaded of the error of his views, and abandoning his tenets and position as an adwaitic Sanyasin, voluntarily chose to be converted under name of *Govinda Yati* and counted himself among his supporters. He composed a work on the duties of Sanyasins (*Yatidharma Samuchchaya*) which exists to this day. We have no means of ascertaining whether this Yadavaprakasa is identical with the one mentioned in the Bhashya and later works, as the author of the *Bheda-abheda* doctrine allied to the Bhaskara school; but tradition asserts that the two are identical. There is no allusion in any of the existing lives of Ramanuja that the Yadavaprakasa under whom he studied and whom he later on converted was anything put a pure adwaitin of the Sankara School. If this Yadava had developed a new philosophy materially differing from Sankara's, it is strange that no allusion is made to that fact in the existing lives. It is, however, certain that

Ramanuja did controvert and defeat a Yadavaprakasa in his life-time, for both Anthrapurna, contemporary and disciple of Ramanuja, and Vedanta Desika, a follower of Ramanuja, who lived in the 14th century, testify to the truth of this fact in their respective works, laudatory of Ramanuja.

To proceed. At this juncture Ramanuja had another call from Srirangam which he, willing to take his place as the leader of the community, gladly accepted, and started south. He took Dasarathi with him and reaching the outskirts of Srirángam was met in advance by an eager concourse of devotees who took him in procession to the quarters intended for him and installed him formally as their spiritual superior in the seat of Yamunacharya. Meanwhile an incident happened to Kuresa which led him to abandon his riches and migrate to Srirangam followed by his wife. This was nothing less than a report at Conjeevaram that the rumbling noise of his huge palatial gates closing at nights disturbed the God at Kanchi. Kuresa was ashamed of the vanity which the rumour implied and abandoning all his wealth to the poor, went with nothing but the clothes he wore and his wife similarly clad, to join Sri Ramanuja at Srirangam. There he adopted the life of a mendicant and lived on the alms which he begged from day to day. It was also now that Ramanuja was gladdened by the news of the conversion of Govinda Bhatta, his cousin and fellow pupil, who had all this time been a staunch Saivite, doing service in the Kalahasti temple. His uncle Sri Saila, at Ramanuja's request, converted him after some trouble and brought him over to Tirupati. Later, he joined Ramanuja, assumed the garb of a Sanyasin and became an important disciple under the name of Embar.

About this time Ramanuja defeated in controversy and also converted an adwaitic scholar, Yagnamurti by name. who became a Sanyasin on his defeat and Ramanuja's disciple under the style of Devaraja Muni.

Even before the date of some of these conversions, Ramanuja had himself to study patiently, after joining the Srirangam Mutt, under various teachers, who were the pupils of Yamunacharya, and specially held in reserve, as it were, instructions intended for Ramanuja. One of them was Goshtipurna, who, after trying Ramanuja eighteen times by compelling him to travel all the way from Srirangam to the Madura District, where his place was, at last deigned, after exacting promises of secrecy, to impart to him certain important teachings. Ramanuja once in possession of them, straightway called together a group of men and proclaimed loudly the truths he learned with so much difficulty. The furious guru asked him to explain his conduct, and Ramanuja said that he did not care if perdition was his fate for the transgression, but that he valued more the saving of men's souls. Thus did Ramanuja open out the hearts of even his conservative teachers and prepare the way for the breakdown of narrow prejudices. The other teachers of Ramanuja also found that he had more to teach them than they had to impart. Such were Maladhara and his uncle Sri Sailapurna. The latter instructed him in the truths of the Ramayana in the course of an extended visit of nearly a year which Ramanuja spent at Tirupati for the purpose.

Ramanuja now thought of composing philosophical works and committing to writing the special views which he was developing orally. One of the first works that he composed was the *Vedartha Sangraha* wherein he tackled the principal Upanishads that lent themselves to adwaitic interpretation, established the unsoundness of such interpretation, and expounded his own views. The very first of such passages is the famous one of the Chandogya Upanishad wherein occurs the enigmatic sentence, '*Tat twam asi*,' 'that thou art' which is the corner-stone of all adwaitic expositions. He also attacks in this work the doctrine of Maya of Sankara, and the Bheda-abheda doctrines of the Bhaskara and Yadava schools. Then he sets out his view of the ultimate truths and gives his method of reconciling Vedic passages. He then takes up the question, of great religious importance to Hindus, and a matter of severe contention in disputations, whether the Supreme Deity is to be styled Narayana or is to be identified with Siva or some of the other Gods known to the Upanishads, and concludes by establishing that the former alone is explicitly named as the Deity in both his personal and impersonal forms. This controversy of names, it will be seen, is independent of the dispute between Adwaitism and Visishtadwaitism and there are plenty of confirmed adwaitins to whom God as Vishnu or Narayana is the object of worship.

Ramanuja now addressed himself to his *magnum opus*, the Bhashya on the Vedanta Sutras. We have explained on a previous occasion that Ramanuja's interpretation followed the *Bodhayana Vritti*, a very early gloss on the Sutras composed long before Sankara's time and essentially representative of the very views which Ramanuja expounded. To get at the manuscript of the *Vritti*, which was unavailable in Southern India, Ramanuja, it is said, had to travel to Kashmir with Kuresa and other pupils. With considerable difficulty, he obtained permission to read the manuscript but not to take any copy of the same. Kuresa of wonderful memory committed to heart important passages in the simple act of reading them once and relieved Ramanuja of all anxiety as to his being unable to make a copy of the work and take it with him. The party then returned to Srirangam and Ramanuja composed the Bhashya, Kuresa being the amanuensis. It seems that Kuresa, who remembered the *Vritti*, never actively suggested any objection to Ramanuja's exposition, but where any error crept in, in the nature of a disagreement with the *Vritti*, he simply would not write down any further, and Ramanuja took the hint and usually amended the text. We have clear testimony that Ramanuja had access to passages in the *Vritti* before he composed the Bhashya, and it is also unlikely that he went all the way to Kashmir once for the purpose of seeing the manuscript and again during the course of the long tour round the Peninsula to be mentioned later on and before which he is said to have completed the Bhashya. The fact may be that Ramanuja procured the *Vritti* from some library in the North, but not from Kashmir; or perhaps his reference to stray passages was from traditional quotations and he really was enabled to verify his references only at Kashmir; or lastly, we may suppose that the work was really composed after his return from his long trip and Ramanuja utilised the study of the *Vritti* in the composition. The Sri Bhashya is the work of a mature intellect, and there is nothing improbable in supposing that Ramanuja's views, settled by the ordeal of frequent controversies during his trip, were committed to writing, after his return, in deliberation.

After the composition of the Sri Bhashya, Ramanuja composed two epitomés of the same, a short one, the *Vedanta Sara* containing the Sutras and a simple gloss, and the *Vedanta Dipa*, a work on the same model, but fuller in discussion and exposition. Both works are valuable aids to the study of the Sutras and deserve to be better known, though it must be admitted that they are thoroughly eclipsed by the masterly *Sri Bhashya*. Ramanuja also composed a commentary on the Bhagavat-Gita, known as the *Gita Bhashya*, a work of great merit, the result of considerable thought, which has since been amply expounded by the classical commentary *Tatparya Chandrika* of Sri Vedanta Desika. The other works of Ramanuja are the *Gadya-traya* and the *Nitya*, works devoted to practical religious purposes and requiring no further notice.

The grand trip of Ramanuja round the Peninsula now requires mention. With a large following of disciples and with the express object of visiting various shrines and incidentally controverting opposition to his views, wherever it may arise, Ramanuja started from Srirangam. He first travelled east, visited Kumbhakonam and the shrines of the Shiyali Taluk near the scene of Thirumangai Alwar's birth. He then turned south and visited the shrines of Madura and Tinnevelly and in the latter district visited Alwar-Tirunagari and the neighbouring shrines where St. Sadagopa was born and lived. From here he went to Rameswaram. Returning to Tirunagari, he went to Malabar and Travancore, visited various Vishnu shrines scattered over these places and then marched northwards along the seacoast to Girnar and Dwaraka in Guzerat, where Sri Krishna lived and ruled. Thence he went to Muttra, Govarthan, etc., places sacred to the memory of Sri Krishna. From these he went further north up the Himalayas to Badarinath. He then visited Kashmir and stopped at Srinagar, where he is said to have been challenged by Saraswati herself, the Goddess of learning.

The text which Ramanuja was asked to expound at Srinagar was the famous passage in Chandogya, I 6.7. "*Yatha Kapyasam pundarikam Evan Akshini*" lt. "As is the *Kapyasa* lotus, so were his eyes." The word *Kapyasa* has been interpreted by Sankaracharya as the "posteriors of the monkey." Sankara gave this apparently literal interpretation, unaware of any other traditional interpretation, and excused the obvious awkwardness of the comparison by saying that it was only a simile subsidiary to another simile and was, therefore, of no harm. His meaning of the text would thus be, "The eyes of the Deity were like the lotus which resembled the (red) posteriors of the monkey." It will be seen that, apart from the unseemly comparison, Sankara requires the interpolation of another word 'like' for which the text gives no room. The text naturally implies that 'kapyása' is co-ordinate with 'pundarika'. Ramanuja therefore abandoned Sankara's meaning and interpreted *kapi* to mean the sun' or 'the rays of the sun'. This derivative meaning had been suggested to him by one of the early commentators, the Vakyakara Tanka, referred to before in the life of Yamunacharya, who interpreted 'kapyasa', as 'full-blown by the rays of the sun'.* Ramanuja improved upon this interpretation by exhausting the possibilities of derivative construction afforded by the word and which seemed suited to the context. His full explanatory meaning as given in the *Vedartha Sangraha*, (see p. 234 of the Benares Edition and the commentary thereon) is as follows:—The eyes of the Deity were beautiful "like a (red) lotus, *grown in deep water, standing on a strong stalk, and full-blown by the rays of the sun*"† We need hardly say that a com-

* *Aditya-Kshipta.*

†See also the Upanishad Commentary of Rangaramanuja Muni, Madras Telugu Edition, Chandogya, page 30, for a full exposition of this passage. Also *Srutaprakasika* (p. 458, Vol. I, Grantha Edition) on the Sri Bhashya at I. 1. 21.

munity which sets so much store by the personal aspect of God would consider a construction like Sankara's as an affront to Him, though of course Sankara intended no such thing and only followed an apparent popular meaning of the word '*kapi*.'

This interpretation of Ramanuja thoroughly satisfied Saraswati, we are told, and She blessed him and his Bhashya. Ramanuja, however, roused the ire of the adwaitic pandits of the place, who, defeated in open controversy, tried to encompass his life by dark means. Ramanuja and his party, however, escaped and descending the Himalayas, proceeded to Benares. From Benares he travelled south-east and reached Puri or Jagannath on the eastern coast and established a mutt there. Unable to introduce his mode of temple worship at Puri owing to the opposition of the priests, he left the place and proceeded to Tirupati. Here occurred what is considered a miracle in connection with the God of the Seven Hills. A dispute was raging at the time of Ramanuja's visit as to whether the God was Vishnu or Siva. It is claimed by the Vaishnavas that the God was Vishnu in the times preceding that of Ramanuja, as the Saiva saints dedicated no stanzas to him, though neighbouring Siva shrines were noticed. It also appears that in the times of an early Alwar who preceded St. Sadagopa, the God is described as wearing both Vaishnavite and Saivite symbols. A fruitful source of dispute seems to have existed in the place based on this dual aspect. It may be that in Ramanuja's tim there was a fresh attempt to oust the Vaishnavites.

was now suggested that both Vishnu and Siva symbols should be placed before the God at night and that the decision as to the God's nature should follow any indication that He may give in the matter. This was done by Ramanuja and the people of the place, with the result that, early next morning, the God was seen wearing the discus and the conch, the symbols of Vishnu, to the neglect of the symbols of Siva also placed before him. Thus ended a controversy which has never cropped up again.

From Tirupati Ramanuja travelled south, visiting Conjeevaram, Tirukoilur, and Tiruvahidrapuram (Cuddalore) and lastly Viranarayanapuram, the birthplace of Nathamuni. He then reached Srirangam after completing successfully an extended tour of several years, during which he acquired great fame and largely increased his influence.

His life at Srirangam need not be described in detail. With great tact and ability he managed through his disciples the affairs of the Srirangam Temple entrusted to him, and at the same time instructed his followers and ministered to their spiritual wants. Hundreds of eminent men and women surrounded him and hung upon his words. His congregation included, we are told, 700 Sanyasins, 74 dignitaries holding special offices of ministry, and innumerable holy men and women who revered him as God. Ramanuja was now an aged man near 70, but was destined to live many years more and instruct his contemporaries. He was fond of his disciples and they reciprocated the feeling. One of them, a son of Sri Saila his uncle, was bred up as a son to him and named Kurukesa, after St. Sadagopa, in fulfilment of the pledge to Yamuna's spirit, which we have mentioned before.

By the composition of the Sri Bhashya, he had redeemed another of the pledges. The third pledge was redeemed by Ramanuja naming a son of his friend Kuresa as Parasara, the name of the saintly father of Vyasa and the author of the Vishnupurana, which is held in great esteem. Kurukesa, otherwise named Pillan, composed a monumental, though brief, commentary called the Six thousand, on the 1,000 stanzas of the Tiruvai Mozhi, of St. Sadagopa. Parasara Bhattar, son of Kuresa, was a brilliant man, almost a prodigy and has composed various works, one of them being a commentary on the *Sahasranama* called *Bhagavad-guna Darpana.*

Troublous days were in store for Ramanuja. The Chola King (Kulothungachola I), persuaded by the bigoted Saivites of his Court, sent for Ramanuja to ask him for a subscription of his faith in Siva as the Supreme Lord. Kuresa, personating Ramanuja, accepted the summons, wore his master's red robes and went in his place, accompanied by the aged Mahapurna, Ramanuja's earliest teacher. The two reached the Court of the monarch (at Chidambaram in all probability,) and attempting to argue out the superiority of Vishnu, were commanded by the cruel monarch to have their eyes extracted. This was done and the unfortunate pair stumbled out somehow and started for Srirangam. On the way Mahapurana died, unable to bear the pangs of pain, and Kuresa reached Srirangam alone. Finding the place closed to Vaishnavites, he repaired to Madura where he lived near the shrine of Tirumalirunjolai, a Vishnu temple of great sanctity.

Meanwhile Ramanuja with a sprinkling of his followers left Srirangam in fear of persecution and by hurried and nightly marches reached the outskirts of the Nilgiri hills. After great difficulties and many adventures, the party travelled across the forests, and reached Vahnipushkarini, a place on the Kaveri about 40 miles west of Mysore. Thence the party went east, halting at Mirle and Saligram, about 10 miles eastwards. Here Ramanuja spent some time converting a large number, and one Anthrapurna among the rest, who became a devoted follower thereafter. The party then reached Tonnur or Tondanur, where then resided the King Bitti Deva, of the Hoysala dynasty, whose capital was Dwara Samudra or the modern Halbeid. These events may be assigned to about the year 1088 or 1089 A. D., when Ramanuja was over 70 years old. The Rajah's daughter was possessed and the King and Queen were sore distressed on that account. A common acquaintance suggested Ramanuja as capable of exorcising the devil by the power of his austerities. Ramanuja was invited to the place and luckily succeeded in curing the Princess of her malady. The King and Queen were greatly pleased. Ramanuja, taking advantage of an affront which the Jain community to which the

King belonged had offered to the latter, converted him to Vaishnavism and changed his name to Vishnuvardhana.

A great disputation followed between the Jains and Ramanuja in which Ramanuja won a complete victory. It is said that Ramanuja, plied with the impatient questions of thousands of Jains on all sides, got inside a curtain, and assuming the form of a thousand-headed Adisesha, answered each one, individually and so effectively, that the clamorous rabble fled away in terror. The story goes that the zealous convert King ground a large number of his quondam co-religionists in oil-mills, despoiled them of all their land-grants, erased their temples, and otherwise maltreated them. These statements of course must be taken with a considerable grain of salt, as it is very unlikely that any politic prince would have raised so unnecessarily such an opposition from his own people. Ramanuja established himself in Tonnur and had a large and beautiful lake constructed out of the waste materials of the despoiled Jaina shrines; the lake exists to this day and is called the *moti talab* or the lake of pearls.

Ramanuja's stay in Mysore extended over nearly twenty years. He succeeded in creating a strong and learned Vaishnavite community whose descendants exist to this day. He built the temple of Vishnu at Melukote or Tirunarayanapuram, a few miles north of Mysore, and established in it the God Narayana whose statue was discovered by him on the spot, from the revelations of a dream. He also recovered a copper idol, Ramapriya, of the same God, which he learned, also from a dream, to be with a Muhammadan princess at Delhi and procured it, after an arduous journey to that place. The panchamas of the place were of great help to him in this business and he assigned them in gratitude certain limited rights of entry into the temple on fixed days, which privilege is enjoyed by them to this day. He then set up, with the help of his disciples, various other images at Belur and other places, and established a procedure for worship on a firm basis in all of them. He resumed his religious instruction, as at Srirangam in peace and serenity, enjoying the favour of the ruler and the devotion of his old and new followers. He went to Padmagiri, (Sravana Belgola) the Buddhistic stronghold, and there obtained victories in argument over the Buddhists of the place and converted a large number.

Meanwhile news had reached him that the Chola King who persecuted him was no more, having fallen a victim to a serious carbuncle. He also heard of the misfortune of Kuresa and the death of his venerable teacher, Mahapurna. Sorely grieved, he longed to return to Srirangam, and console Kuresa and his numerous old followers. He, therefore, implored his Mysore friends to let him depart, which they did after getting an exact image of Ramanuja, which they set up for worship. He then started for Srirangam and reached it, travelling in rapid marches in the company of a large group of disciples. The people of Srirangam welcomed him with open hearts and conducted him to his mutt in triumphal procession, The successor of Kulothunga I was a pro-Vaishnava ruler and Ramanuja was left undisturbed. Ramanuja met his affectionate follower Kuresa, now blind and decrepit, and shed tears of the deepest sorrow over his misfortunes.

Yet another journey awaited Ramanuja in his last days. Learning that the God Govindaraja, removed from Chidambaram under the orders of the late Chola ruler, was preserved in concealment at Tirupati, he journeyed to that place and established a shrine for that deity at the foot of the hills. He then returned to Srirangam and resumed his saintly life. After some more years of useful work, he closed his long and active career quietly at Srirangam, in the year 1137 A. D., having lived for 120 years, a span of life unusual among men, but which, we are assured from all accounts, was a historical fact in his case.

It must be added that his devoted follower Kuresa died a few years previously, deeply mourned by Ramanuja himself and by all around him.

That Ramanuja's was an exemplary character needs no demonstration. There are various incidents in his life (which space forbids us to mention) that bring out his broad-mindedness, burning sympathy for mankind, unselfishness to an extraordinary degree, resourcefulness and absolute devotion to God. He went further than any other Vaidic teacher in recognising merit even though combined with socially inferior birth. He was an able interpreter of the human heart, and won men and women of different temperaments to the path of religion by suitable sympathetic treatment. His writings show the keenness of his intellect, the vastness of his learning, and the sincerity and seriousness of his character. His moderation in controversy is remarkable. He has no harsh word anywhere for his opponents. His work on the practical side is truly epoch-making. His disciples were the ancestors of innumerable Vaishnava families throughout the Presidency who deem it their highest honour that they are so descended. That the Vishnu temples are places of large resort and centres of social and religious influence, is due entirely to his initiative and prudent fore-thought. Abuses creep into the best institutions and they can hardly be ascribed to the originators in any case. Ramanuja's religious activity bore fruit even outside the Presidency. In distant Bengal, a pupil of his was succeeded by the well-known Ramanand who preached Vaishnavaism and Bhakti, and has created many thousands professing the Vaishnava cult in Bengal and other parts of the North. Ramanuja, preceded and followed as he was by various reformers of eminence in his own line, is rightly held to be the founder of the Visishtadwaitic system, a brief description of which will now conclude this sketch of Ramanuja's Life.

II

Philosophy of Ramanujacharya.

THE TERM 'VISISHTADWAITA' EXPLAINED.

THE Visishtadwaita is so called because it inculcates the *adwaita* or oneness of God, with *visesha* or attributes. It is, therefore, 'qualified non dualism.' God alone exists; all else that is seen is His manifestation, attribute, or *Sakti*. Such attributes are *chit* or the individual souls and *achit* or matter. The adwaitic position is also that God alone exists and all else is manifestation. Herein is the common element between the two views; but the Adwaitin regards the manifestation as unreal and temporary, and as a result of *Avidya* or Nescience. In consequence, the one Brahman is without any attribute, in his view. Ramanuja and his school regard the attributes as real, and permanent, but subject to the control of the one Brahman in all their modifications and evolutions. The oneness of God is compatible with the existence of attributes, as the latter are incapable of existing alone, and so do not constitute independent things. They are called the *prakaras* or the modes, *sesha* or the accessories, and *niyamya* or the controlled, of the one Brahman. The word Brahman is thus used either to denote the central unity, when it becomes possible to speak of the souls and matter, as its attributes, or to denote the combined trinity when the whole universe may properly be described as consisting of Brahman and Brahman alone. The Visishtadwaitin does not make the unphilosophical statement that the souls are absolutely independent entities, endowed with the capacity of separate existence and activity, apart from Brahman.

THE FUNDAMENTAL ATTRIBUTES.

The Brahman (we use the word in the first of the above senses) is Intelligence. It is something more—it is the Knower. Where attributes are denied, and all that exists is homogenous intelligence, as in the Adwaita, there can be no knower; for there is nothing to know. But for the Visishtadwaitin, Brahman is a knower. and the variety, philosophically essential for knowledge, is furnished by the attributes. Brahman is Bliss, *i.e.*, he is blissful; for a mixture of the opposite, pain, is unimaginable in his case. It will thus be seen that besides the attributes of souls and matter, which may be called 'the concrete attributes' if such a phrase may be used, Brahman has various abstract attributes, qualities strictly so-called, denoting his perfection from various points of view. The Visishtadwaitin considers 'Intelligence' as partaking of the dual character of an abstract and a concrete attribute; and he instances 'light' as an example of the possibility of such an attribute. Intelligence, is of the essence of Brahman; it is an attribute as well, in its nature of universal pervasion. Again Brahman is real, *satya*. By this is understood that he is without *vikara* or modifications of any kind. The souls and matter are *asatya* or unreal, which again means that they are subject to modification, which is necessarily an element of impurity. In the case of souls, this modification takes the form of expansion or contraction of Intelligence. In mineral, plant, or animal life, the soul under *karmic* control, is dull or of suppressed Intelligence. The modifications of matter are of a more serious kind. In the creation and expansion of the universe, matter undergoes a real modification of its nature. Such change is called *parinama* or evolution as contrasted with *vivarta* or apparent variation, which is the view of the Adwaitin. The Visishtadwaitin holds that, in spite of the souls and matter being pervaded by Brahman, any modification of them, though under Brahman's control, do not touch His essence; just as the Adwaitin maintains that the operations of *Avidya* do not affect the one Reality. The 'unreality' of the cosmos is thus another point of agreement between the Adwaitin and the Visishtadwaitin; but this, it must be admitted, is merely a nominal agreement, considering the important diversity in their conceptions of the unreality. The Visishtadwaitin would thus call Brahman, '*Sat*,' and the rest '*Asat*': in a narrower sense, he reserves the epithet 'Asat' to Matter, which undergoes change in its essence, unlike the souls whose essence is like to the Brahman's and never changes.

TWO STATES OF BRAHMAN.

There are two states of existence for the Brahman. One is absolute quiescence or *pralaya*, when all the souls and matter exist in Him in deep sleep as it were. No differentiation is possible in that stage between the souls and matter; these are then, as it were, non-existent. '*Sat* alone exists, one without a second.' Existence is the only phrase that can be applied to the Brahman then, as volition, not to speak of creation, is potential or has not commenced to work. Then begins the second stage, creation. To the Adwaitin, creation is a negative, an unreal, act. It is the clouding of the pure Intelligence of Brahman by the inexplicable Avidya, which produces the manifestation of apparent diversity. The Visishtadwaitin considers creation as a positive volitional effort of the Brahman to display real diversity, by actualising the energy for change which is innate in both the souls and matter. *Sa Aikshta bahu syam prajayeya iti.* 'He thought, may I become many, may I grow forth.' The *antah pravesa* 'entry within' which the Upanishads speak of as taking place at creation is not strictly true. To the Visishtadwaitin, it means only the Brahman's willing to develop his inseparable attributes, souls and matter; for Brahman was 'within' even before creation. To the Adwaitin, the *antah pravesa* is entirely metaphorical. The language of the *Parinama Vada* is used in his view merely for facility of comprehension.

THE PURPOSE OF CREATION.

The ethical justification for creation is Justice.

The fruits of actions (karma) have to be bestowed, equally and impartially, and Brahman does this by endowing souls with appropriate bodies of various kind and giving room for further functioning and display of free will within limits; the further evolution depends on the manner in which the individual uses his opportunities. As karma is, in the Hindu view, beginningless, it becomes unnecessary to account for its origin. To the objection that Brahman could have no purpose, being without wants, in engaging itself in creation, the reply is, in the words of the author of the Sutras, *lokavat tu lila-kaivalyam* (II. 1.33), it is mere recreation, as in ordinary life. In other words, as no compulsion can be predicated of the Brahman to evolve the universe, the Visishtadwaitin accounts for it by the only other possible alternative, that it is mere recreation for the Brahman, but the strictest justice for the souls concerned. Sankara adds the explanation that His innate nature (*svabhava*) is to create, which does not carry us much further, and then reminds us that the whole discussion is unreal, as Brahman is never the agent of creation.

THE AUTHORITY OF REVELATION.

To the Visishtadwaitin, as to the Adwaitin, the Vedas and Smritis are the sole and independent authority for the knowledge of Brahman. Reason has no operation except in matters perceptible by the senses. Transcendental notions as those with respect to the nature and attributes of Brahman and the souls, can only be got from Revelation. This position appears illogical, dethroning, as it does, *Reason*, the accepted instrument of correct conclusion in all processes of thought. To explain this anomaly, we have to dwell a little on the exact place assigned to reason by Sankara as well as Ramanuja. Reason is an indefinite word. It depends for its correctness, on the intellectual capacity of the person arguing, the extent of his information and other circumstances. Until a fallacy is exposed, an argument is apparently sound. Then it is upset and the conclusion is to be reached by other reasonings. This want of finality in mere reason is referred to in the Sutras (II-1-11) and is the cause of the Vedantic systems rejecting it as a sufficient authority in the knowledge of Brahman as the Nyayikas did. The argument from design may at best establish a highly endowed intelligent first cause or causes, but could not lead to the conception of a perfect Brahman as first cause. And so, the help of mere reason as a sufficiently competent determining factor in the establishment of Brahman, as first cause, is rejected. This must not be taken to mean that the Hindu Vedantins reject argumentation in their philosophy. Every page of their writings is a standing monument of their skill in the subtlest reasonings. According to them the purpose of reasoning is two-fold. It has, in the first place, full scope in matters which do not transcend the senses. In the second place, it is a valuable adjunct in ontology, where the texts of the Vedas are to be construed. As it so happens that most important texts are liable to be disputed as to their meanings, it goes without saying that there is full room for logical interpretation with respect to them. To say that explicit Vedic texts are unquestionable authorities means one of two things, either that we take them as the conclusions of great minds reached after acute reasoning, on matters which our feeble intellects could not sufficiently comprehend, or we consider them to be the records of unique direct experiences of men who had trained their powers of mental perception by methods to which we have no access. Neither position is inconceivable or necessarily absurd. So many scientific positions are accepted by the general body of educated men all over the world on the faith of representations that those positions have been verified by some one by actual experiments. There may be danger of mis-statements in either case; but those like Sankara and Ramanuja, who do not feel the position of an agnostic satisfactory or comfortable, have preferred to base their ontological position on revelation, while fully trusting to their capacity for ratiocination to meet objections on the part of those who do not subscribe to the authority of the Vedas. Between these two, there is, however, a difference. Sankara includes the Srutis and Smritis among ephemeral things whose purpose is served when once oneness is realised. Ramanuja considers them as always authoritative and as expressive of the eternal commands of the deity whose breath they are said to be. An important difference arises between these two thinkers, based on this distinction. In Sankara's view the compulsory nature of ordained duties lasts only till an individual has realised by thinking his unity with God. Ramanuja considers the performance of such duties obligatory as long as life and physical power endure. (See Sutras III. 4.32-35.)

There are also certain assertions in Ramanuja's religious tenets which must be unacceptable to those who do not believe in revelation or adopt his interpretation. Such are his eternally free souls (*nityas*), heaven conceived as a distinct place apart from and outside the changeable universe (though not outside Brahman), the existence of the Deity in physical forms of various kinds, the peculiar path of souls on their release from the body, and so on. Belief in these is based on express texts and no reasoning can be called to prove them. It is Ramanuja's contention that reasoning is equally powerless to disprove them. And a disapproval of these in no way affects Ramanuja's conclusions, as regards the nature of Brahman and its relation to souls and matter, as philosophical positions consonant to abstract reasoning.

MODE OF RECONCILIATION.

We now come to Ramanuja's mode of reconciling Vedic texts. Western scholars have tried to arrange chronologically the principal Upanishads and to discern, in some of them, partial truths; in others, crude statements; in others again, the completest insight into things transcendental that may be given to man. How far this discussion is convincing we shall not stop to examine. Where passages in the same Upanishads appear to conflict, as in the *Chandogya*, the *Brihad-Aranyaka*, or the *Isa-Vasya*, it is evident that the ordinary rules of interpretation must be resorted to, to arrive at a consistent meaning. The respect which Hindus have entertained for the Upanishads on account of their antiquity has prevented them from considering any of them as of inferior authority to the rest. It follows that a consistent doctrine has to be attempted out of at least the principal Upanishads. This is what Sankara and Ramanuja have attempted to do, each in his own way. And this is indeed what Badarayana, the first interpreter of the Upanishads known to us, has himself done in the Sutras.

Professor Deusson and others have conjectured that Badarayana had a partiality for the Chandogya and hence the frequent reference to it in the topics discussed, Indian scholars thoroughly equipped with an intimate acquaintance with "the immense and highly technical philosophical literature, which is only just beginning to be studied and comprehended, in part, by European scholars," to use the words of Dr. Thibaut, have ascertained that, in the two Mimamsas, the passages discussed in each Adhikarana are only typical and not exhaustive and that the order of exposition is mainly based on logical sequence. It follows that there is justification for the view that one or two Upanishads are specially intended as the repositary of philosophical truths to the exclusion of other Upanishads.

The texts of the Upanishads referring to the supreme Self are of two kinds. Some speak of Him as *nirguna*, attributeless. Others describe him as having attributes or qualities like wisdom, power, etc. As truth can be only one, the natural question arises whether these texts can be reconciled in any manner. Sankara's view is that predominance must be given to the *nirguna* texts, as the others have the effect of limiting the Infinite, which should not be done. Hence texts like '*Ekam eva Adwaitiyam*,' one only, without a second,' *neha nana Asti*,' there is here no diversity, etc., are interpreted by him, without much straining, as establishing the absolute one-ness of the Brahman. And the other texts are relegated to an inferior position and made to refer to an imaginary and inferior Brahman called *apara* or *karya* Brahman, *i.e.*, the Brahman in conjunction with its creative power called *maya*. Ramanuja's difficulty seems to be that this sharp division of the passages into those referring to the higher and those referring to the lower Brahman is not easily and directly inferable from the texts themselves. On the other hand, the passages are so mixed up that it is impossible to say that this distinction, if true, was ever prominently kept up. His reconciliation is, therefore, as follows: the texts of the Upanishads do not inculcate an attributeless Brahman; the attributes are real and not the result of Avidya; the texts referring to these attributes expound the Brahman as He is, with the souls and matter as His inseparable *modes*. Brahman is one, only in His compound nature, as described already. The texts denying any attributes for Him are to be taken as meaning that He has no low or inauspicious attributes, such as liability to changes, death, sorrow, etc. The texts as to creation, as mentioned already, mean a real modification of the attributes, souls and matter of the Brahman and do not mean that Brahman becomes suffused with Nescience and imagines a variety. The souls are many and God is immanent, both in them and in matter. The texts which speak of unity and deny variety do so of the totality of the Brahman with his attributes. Texts, which deny a second to Brahman, mean that there is no other controlling power in the universe apart from Him. Texts which deny the possibility of knowing Brahman, do not mean that he cannot be the object of thought, as there is no thinker; they mean only that His wonderful and priceless excellences or qualities could not be adequately described. Else, according to Ramanuja, they would conflict with hosts of passages which prescribe knowledge of Brahman and ascribe qualities to Him. The text of the Brihad Aranyaka II. 3. 6. which contains the famous words "*neti neti.*" "not so, not so" and is taken by Sankara to teach the negation of all attributes, is interpreted by Ramanuja (Sutras. III. 22.1) as merely denying the possibility of adequate knowledge of the Brahman. "This interpretation," says he, "is confirmed by the fact that after the negative phrase come an epithet of Brahman as 'the True of the True. for the Pranas are the True'." Ramanuja interprets this text to mean that the Pranas or the individual souls are *satya* or 'true' *i.e.*, not subject to change in their essence, while the supreme Self is altogether real or unchangeable. "He is, therefore, more eminently *true* than they (the souls) are.'

THE THEORY OF CAUSATION.

The theory of causation has profoundly exercised the minds of all Hindu philosophers; the Vedantins, like the Sankhyas, maintain the oneness of cause and effect in essence, as opposed to the logicians who maintain that they are different. In what sense, then, is the world which is an effect, one with its cause? Badarayana has a topic discussing this point. (Sutras, 1. IV. 23. etc.) Here he maintains that the Brahman is not merely the instrumental cause, but also the material cause of the universe. He is, in the position, not merely of the potter but also of the mud, to give an illustration familiar to Indian philosophers. A succeeding Sutra, (I. 4. 27.) refers to the way in which Brahman as the cause becomes the effect. It is by *parinama*' or owing to modification. In Ramanuja's view the oneness of cause and effect arises from the fact that the cause is the Brahman in the *sûkshma* or subtle state, when the souls and matter are undeveloped and the effect is Brahman also, now comprised of the Supreme Self and the souls and matter, the latter in a fully developed state. Sankara, practically admitting the interpretation of the Sutras given above, would, however, explain the modification as '*Vivarta*' really *i.e.*, phenomenal creation by Brahman as influenced by Avidya or Maya. That the two philosophers are entirely at variance in their view of this oneness is also clear from their respective commentaries on the important Sutra II-1-15, (14. in Sankara's numbering a discussion of which would be out of place in this brief exposition. We would only draw attention to an important and suggestive statement of Sankaracharya, at the close of his commentary of the above Sutra. that Badarayana, in his view, omits to contradict the reality of the manifested world and adopts the language of the *Parinâma Vada*, for the purpose of facilitating the exposition of the saguna meditations later on in the work.

THE DOCTRINE OF NESCIENCE.

Ramanuja's Sribhashya is remarkable for the lengthy disquisition on various topics by which his actual commentary on the Sutras is preceded. In this disquisition, he treats of various controversial points and expounds fully his differences of views from those of Sankara. One of the most important of these is his statement of objections to the theory of Maya or Avidya, which is a fundamental one in Sankara's philosophy and is, at the same time, the most vulnerable point in it. Is this Avidya different from or identical with Brahman? The former view would seem to undermine Sankara's doctrine of oneness and the latter is equally untenable. Sankara cuts the Gordian knot, by boldly declaring that it (the Avidya) is *Sadasadanirvachaniya*. *i.e.*, it is indescribable as either existing or non-existing. Ramanuja expounds at great length his difficulties as to the tenability of the Maya theory, under seven heads, a clear account of which is to be found in Professor Ranghacharya's 'Analytical outline' prefixed to his valuable translation of the Sri Bashya, Vol. I. Ramanuja's objections are of this wise: The Avidya cannot operate on the Brahman, directly, for His nature is Intelligence and this would repel Nescience by its intrinsic merit. Nor can it operate on the individual souls, for these are the outcome of the action of Avidya and cannot, therefore, be acted upon in anticipation. Again, to state that Nescience clouds the Brahman is impossible, for that would mean that Brahman's luminous nature is thereby destroyed, a position which is not admissible. Avidya, again, as defined by Sankara, is in Ramanuja's view, inconceivable, as the simultaneous possession of two opposite characters as existence and non-existence, cannot be predictaed of anything in human conception. Ramanuja, further, does not think that to describe Avidya as 'indescribable' really strengthens the position of Sankara; for if a thing is absolutely indescribable, it must be non-existent as an entity. Then Ramanuja points out that such an Avidya cannot be proved to exist by any known means of proof including Vedic or Smriti texts; if such an Avidya should exist, it is irremovable says Ramanuja, for the knowledge of attributeless Brahman required to remove it, is according to him an impossible thing, such a Brahman not being provable. Lastly, such an Avidya is irremovable for another reason. In Ramanuja's view the ignorance, being the result of Karma can be removed only by enjoined action and meditation. Mere knowledge of Brahman cannot remove it. For all these reasons, Ramanuja concludes that the theory of Maya is untenable and opposed to the tenor of the Vedic texts.

CONCLUSION.

It is not the purpose of this sketch to explain all Ramanuja's objections to Sankaracharya's views. What has been attempted is only the setting forth of Ramanuja's views on important points with just so much reference to the doctrines of Sankara, as is necessary to understand Ramanuja. To really grasp the vital differences between these two eminent philosophers, and to arrive at a proper estimate of their relative merits, would mean a thorough discussion of three important questions, namely, (1) who is the better interpreter of the Upanishads, (2) who has more accurately represented the views of the Vedanta Sutras, and (3) who is entitled to greater respect as a philosophical thinker. These are questions of so difficult a nature that they are entirely beyond our scope and capacity. Enough has, however, been said to show that Ramanuja, when he becomes better known, would most certainly be deemed entitled to a high place among the world's philosophers and his system, though not possessing the simplicity or universality of Sankaracharya's, is yet an eminently sound one, compatible with an admission of the reality of the cosmos and a high conception of the nature and attributes of the Deity.

Sri Vedanta Desika.

———:o:———

THE spread of Vaishnavism in South India after the days of Ramanuja cannot be adequately dealt with in the short space of an article or two. The literature that has come down to us since Ramanuja's days, and which, though not available largely to the general Sanskrit-knowing public, is gradually seeing the light of day in important publications here and there. On the practical side the characteristics of the sect, distinguishing it from the rest of the people, became accentuated in course of time, and an amount of exclusiveness and one-sidedness became the symbol of the class, which cannot but be deplored in its own interests. The spread of Saivism by the advocacy of erudite Sanskrit scholars was a simultaneous feature of these days which has to be taken into account in estimating the cause of this exclusiveness. We have also to mention that a schism of an important nature arose among the followers of Ramanuja in Southern India, a couple of centuries after Ramanuja's death which has only more fully developed itself as days have gone by, and has not contributed, as may be expected, either to enhance the true religious or moral progress of the community as a whole, or to secure the increased respect of the communities around towards the dogmas and practices of the Vaishnavas as a class. It is only necessary to add that we are confining ourselves here to the spread of Vaishnavism in South India, leaving it to a future article to give some account of the prominent features of Vaishnavism as it has developed in Northern India.

The legitimate successor of Ramanuja in his character as head of the Vaishnavite community is said to be Kurukesa, a disciple of Ramanuja, referred to already as the author of a commentary on the Tiruvoymozhi. Another of his pupils, Pranatartihara of the Atreya Gotra, was a beloved nephew of Ramanuja himself, and a great scholar. He had the sole charge of the preparation of Ramanuja's daily food, a function which, as Ramanuja was a sanyasin, could not be discharged by any one indiscriminately. In course of time this Pranatartihara had a great-grandson Ramanuja or Appullar by name. Varada Vishnu Acharya was another of Ramanuja's pupils whose grandson Varadacharya became a learned scholar. The latter studied under one Vishnuchitta, a Solia Brahmin, pupil of Kurukesa, and the author of a learned commentary on the Vishnupurana, the well-known work of Parasara, besides other works. Vishnuchitta lived about the early part of the thirteenth century A.D., a fact accidentally corroborated by a statement of his in his Vishnuparana commentary* that at the time of his composition the forty-fourth century of the Kaliyuga was progressing. Under Varadacharya whose work

* P. 169, L. 14. Madras Telugu Edition of the Vishnupurana with two commentaries.

Tatwasara is now extant, and who was popularly known as Nadadur Ammal, studied the Atreya Ramanuja already mentioned. Many other eminent men studied under him, one of whom may be specially named here. This was Sudarsana Bhatta, a great-grandson of Kuresa, Ramanuja's disciple and friend. This scholar composed various works that have come down to us: the *Srutaprakasika*, a commentary on the Sri Bhashya, modestly named a 'transcript' of his master's notes, but of considerable learning and polemic ability, a commentary on the Upanishads, another on the *Vedartha Sangraha* of Ramanuja, a commentary on the Sri Bhagavata called *Sukapakshiya** and many others.

One day, in the lecture-hall of Varadacharya, Atreya Ramanuja made his appearance accompanied by a young and attractive boy, whom he introduced as his nephew. This was the future Vedanta Desika,† then about five years of age, if the story is to be believed. The boy was called Venkatanatha, and gave even at that time, evidence of his precocity by reciting, in answer to a doubt, the passage last touched upon in the lecture which had temporarily stopped on the advent of the boy. Varadacharya is said to have been

* Our authority for this statement is Manavalamahamunigal, scholar and saint, a very reliable authority in the matter of references; see page 110 of his commentary on the Tatwatraya of Pillai Lokacharya, Tamil Edition.

† Vedanta Desika or (Vedantacharya) lit. Teacher of Vedanta, though originally a title, has practically become by general use the proper name of this scholar, and hence is frequently used in this article instead of Venkatanatha, his real name.

impressed by his powers of retention and intelligence, and to have blessed him in a neat and prophetic Sanskrit verse.* The boy as he grew up was duly instructed by his uncle in all the usual learning of the Vaishnava scholars. He early impressed his contemporaries with his greatness, and a belief grew up, based on the dreams of his parents, that he was an avatar of the God of Tirupati, and that his birth was inspired by the Deity sending out his *Ghanta* or bell for the purpose. This belief was rife even during the life of Venkatanatha, as we see a reference to it in his allegorical drama, the *Sankalpa Suryoda*,† to be subsequently mentioned.

Venkatanatha, it may be mentioned, was born at Tuppul, a suburb of Conjeevaram about the month of September in the year 1268 A. D. His father was Ananthasuri, and his mother Totaramma, sister of Atreya Ramanuja mentioned already. The boy is said to have been born after a visit of the parents to Tirupati and to have therefore been called by the name of the God of that place. Duly instructed by Ramanuja his uncle, the young man became very learned and exemplary in his conduct and was looked upon as the coming leader of the Vaishnava community. After spending some years at Kanchi, his

* उत्प्रेक्ष्यते बुधजनैरुपपत्तिभूम्ना ।
घंटा हरेः समजनिष्ट यदात्मनेति ॥

† प्रतिष्ठापितवेदान्तः प्रतिक्षिप्तबहिर्मतः ।
भूयास्त्रैविद्यमान्यस्त्वं भूरिकल्याणभाजनम् ॥

native place, Venkatanatha travelled south and took up his residence at Tiruvahindrapurâm, near Cuddalore, for some years. His great ability in composition and disputation acquired for him the title of *Kavi Tarkika simha*, lion of poets and logicians. His skill in all arts and handicrafts obtained for him the title of *Sarvatantra Svatantra* or expert in all arts, and later on, the title of *Vedantacharya* or Vedanta Desika was bestowed on him in admiration of his wonderful ability and powers of exposition in the Vedaṇta. To this day, the site of his house at Tiruvahindrapuram is pointed out as evidence of his stay there, and an old, but well-preserved well still exists which he is said to have built *with his own hands* to satisfy an importunate artisan who objected to his title of universal expert! Vedanta Desika composed many works at Tiruvahindrapuram, chiefly *stotras* or hymns of praise on the Deities of the place. One of them is *Achyutta Sataka* in Prakrit, in a highly difficult style, whose affinity with the spoken dialects of the time remains to be investigated. A Tamil work of his the *Paramata Bhanga* is an able and exhaustive review of all known philosophies and systems, about 16 in number, somewhat on the plan of Madhavacharya's *Sarvadarsana Sangraha*, but not, like that work, a mere statement of the doctrines, but a condensed and learned refutation of the tenets of every system other than the Visishtadwaita. It is practically a summary in Tamil of the vast learning contained in the author's Sanskrit works and is useful to those who are not special students of the latter. The *Gopalavimsati* is a popular Sanskrit hymn of 20 stanzas, in perhaps the sweetest language that this learned writer ever employed, on Sri Krishna and his early exploits.

Venkatanatha now returned to Kanchi and spent his time there in instruction and composition. With his usual facility, he composed various hymns on the Deities of that place, the most important of which is the *Varadaraja Panchasat*, on the God at Kanchi, which is a work of considerable merit. Every stanza, as may be expected, bears the impress of his vast learning and deep piety. He also composed here *Nyasadasaka*, a short work on *Prapatti*, the doctrine of surrender, which Vedanta Desika elaborated in numerous later works. He further composed various works in Tamil verse and prose, embodying in easy language the substance of his teachings for the edification of those devoid of Sanskrit learning.

Vedanta Desika now started on his inevitable northern tour. He first visited Tirupati, where he composed and dedicated to the God the work called *Dayasataka*, a hundred and odd stanzas, in long and resounding metres of various kinds, rather harsh in style and obscure in the expression of thought, a combination frequently pervading his more elaborate works, especially of the earlier period.

From Tirupati, Vedanta Desika proceeded northwards and travelled, we are told, through the site of Vijianagar. Vidyaranya, the sanyasin and future Prime Minister of the Vijianagar Kings, had not yet begun his political career. The two met, we are told, and great scholars as both of them were, though of different schools, must have appreciated each other very fully. From Vijianagar, Desika proceeded north to Muttra and Brindavan, and returning, came to Benares passing through Ayodhya on his way. From Benares he turned south-east and followed the usual route of the pilgrims to the eastern coast at Puri or Purushotamam. Thence he turned south, *via* Sri Kurmam, Ahobilam and Tirupati, and reached Kanchi duly, after a prolonged tour of some years. While at Kanchi, we are told, the great Vidyaranya, now a Minister of influence at Vijianagar, sent a message to Vedanta Desika who was reputedly poor, that he could introduce him to royal patronage, if so desired. The reply of Vedanta Desika was short and complete. He cared not for riches or for the favour of kings. His aims and ideals were quite otherwise. The reply was in the form of 5 stanzas, now preserved, which breathe his independence and utter callousness to the charms of wealth. Even if the fact of the message is not historical, we have evidence that Vidyaranya was acquainted with the other's works, as certain verses of Vedanta Desika extracted in Madhava's Sarvadarsana Sangraha* conclusively show. Vijianagar was founded about 1335 and Vedanta Desika may be taken to have been in his fifties during the period of his tour.

Vedanta Desika had now a call from Srirangam where the leading scholar, Sudarsana, above mentioned,

---

* pp. 51 and 53 of the Calcutta Edition of Jibananda.

was getting old, and the doctrines of Vaishnavism badly wanted a defender, learned and powerful. Desika gladly complied, and proceeding to Srirangam rich with the holiest associations as the scene of the labours of Ramanuja and his predecessors, took up his residence there. He how entered upon a vigorous career of instruction and further composition, and produced a number of scholarly and philosophical works, expounding the Visishtadwaita doctrines and combating the views of other schools. He is said to have expounded the Sri Bhashya 30 times and on the 28th occasion of his lectures, composed a work called *Tatwatika*, a lengthy commentary on the Sri Bhashya, a part of which only is now available. He also wrote the *Tatparya Chandrika*, a simple and extensive commentary on the Gita Bhashya Three controversial works were next composed, namely *Satadushani*, *Tatwamukta Kalapa*, and *Nyaya Sidhanjana*. The first is a work of a hundred objections to the Adwaitic views; the second contains, in over 500 verses of flowing metre, a development of the doctrines of the Visishtadwaitic system with refutations of the views of others; while the third is a text book of general philosophy in prose from the Visishtadwaitic point of view.

Vedanta Desika also composed two other important works, one of them the *Seswara mimamsa*, being a direct commentary on the Sutras of Jaimini, where the author tries to show that Jaimini accepted the existence of the Deity, which he is generally supposed not to have done; and the other, the *Adhi-*

karana-saravali, a series of Sanskrit verses in long metre summarising the discussions on the various topics of the Vedanta Sutras. The language of this latter work is simple and clear and shows the great facility which the author possessed in metrical composition on philosophical subjects. The last philosophical work which the author composed is a Tamil Text-book on the Visishtadwaita system and especially its doctrine of *Prapatti*, named the *Rahasyatrayasara*.

It must be mentioned that Vedanta Desika whose works exceed a hundred in number and are in Sanskrit and Tamil on a variety of topics from Geography to *Silpa*, or the practical arts, was a poet of no mean order. He has composed a long and interesting poem, *Yadavabhyudaya*, in 21 cantos, on the life of Sri Krishna, *Sankalpasuryodaya*, an allegorical drama in 10 Acts where Love and Hate and Discrimination, and Ignorance are the *dramatis personae*, a small poem, called *Hamsa sandesa*, in imitation of Kalidasa's 'Meghaduta,' but sufficiently original in conception and delineation, a curious poetical work in very simple language on the sandals of God, *Paduka-Sahasra* by name, and a didactic work of 144 stanzas in his most difficult style, called the *Subhashitanivi*.

All the above works and a number of others in Sanskrit and Tamil were composed by him during his residence at Srirangam where he spent many years of life. His learning and piety, his absolute unselfishness and meekness of character ensured the love of his followers and the respect even of those who differed from his views. His early years were perhaps characterised by an aggressive confidence in his own views and a certain distinct vigour in the expression of them. In later days, he became meek and kind to all and avoided disputations where he could not hope to convince. He created enemies, no doubt, among those Vaishnavaites, who followed other teachers and found differences in the views expounded by him. Such people tried to harass him in various ways. Vedanta Desika however received their insults with meekness and subservience, and tried to unarm hatred and jealousy as far as he could. We have reason to state that the schism in views among the followers of Ramanuja referred to before, commenced about this time and that the teachers, who advocated other views from those of Vedanta Desika, differed from him chiefly in their view of the nature and condition of *Prapatti* or the secret doctrine of surrender to God. Pillai Lokacharya and Peria Achan Pillai were the leading exponents of these views and they have composed works of great learning and ability, mostly in Sanskritised Tamil, indicating fully their views. A pupil in the second generation of the former of these was the great Manavala Mahamuni, a sanyasin of extreme South India, who is the recognised head of the Tengalai sect of the Ramanujiyas, as Sri Vedanta Desika is of the Vadagalai sect. Various differences in practice and doctrines cropped up between these sects, which have become sharper as time passed, and now divides the community into two factions between whom reconciliation seems to be out of the question. We believe however that, even in the days of Manavala Mahamuni, the split was yet a narrow one and we are glad to note that Mànavala Mahamuni himself appreciated Vedanta Desika's merits as he quotes him more than once with approval and usually describes him by the appellation of '*abhiyukta*' which means a respected and reliable author of one's own school. The doctrinal differences between the schools are trivial and are not much appreciated; but we must suppose that the innate love of parading differences is a characteristic of degeneracy in all systems founded on the soundest bases and Vaishnavism has not escaped the general fate of religious doctrines dogmatically carried to excessive detail. It is only a matter of melancholy satisfaction that few practical religions have preserved themselves unsullied by unseemly disputes and schisms as time advances and the inspiration of the original founder ceases to be felt.

We now propose to give some account of our author's allegorical drama, *Sankalpa Suryodaya*, mentioned already. Passion-plays and mystery-plays are well-known in Europe, but seem to be confined to the incidents in the life of Jesus Christ. In Sanskrit literature there are but three principal works* which are dramas of this allegorical nature as far as we know. One of them and possibly the earliest of them is the *Prabodha Chandrodaya*, 'The rise of the moon of knowledge,' by Krishnamisra, who is stated to have lived about the

* *Chaitanya Chandrodaya*, of Karnapura, in addition to the two we are now mentioning.

end of the eleventh century.* Of this work, Professor Macdonell says† that it is "one of the most remarkable products of Indian literature. Though an allegorical play of theologico-philosophical import in which only abstract notions and symbolical figures act as persons, it is full of dramatic power and vigour. It aims at glorifying orthodox Brahminism in the Vaishnava sense just as the allegorical plays of the Spanish poet Calderon were intended to exalt the Catholic faith." The learned scholar's opinion that Prabodha Chandrodaya is a Vaishnava play is accurate, as the express purpose of the play is to exalt the Adwaita faith which cannot be usually identified with Vaishnavism. The play is, however, of moderate proportions in fairly simple style, and the lightness of touch and the humour displayed in exhibiting the practical contrasts among the followers of various tenets show the great dramatic power of the author in fitting for the stage a drama on an abstract subject. The Sankalpa Suryodaya or 'The Rise of the Sun of Divine Will' of Vedanta Desika is a work on the same lines and with a similar purpose, to do for the Vaishtadwaita what Krishnamisra had done for the Adwaita. Vedanta Desika's purpose is to exhibit dramatically the toils and troubles of the human soul before it obtains an insight into Divine Truth, the difficulties in its path of progress to liberation created by passions like Love and Hate, the saving power of Divine grace at every step of this progress,

* His alleged personal interview with Vedanta Desika must, if this date is correct, be only a myth.

† *Vide* page 250, Vol. II, Imperial Gazetteer, Indian Empire.

and the final triumph of the soul over its enemies. The author writes in a serious style, except in some Acts where there is room for humour, and the language is sublime and generally neither harsh nor obscure. The play is rather long and some portions could well have been curtailed, but Sanskrit dramatists, except perhaps Kalidasa, do not do justice to the sense of proportion, and even Bhavabhuti is a sinner in this respect. It has, however, been acted in India and the plot is so contrived that there is enough of action. The reader's, if not the audience's, interest is kept up by sufficient variety of sentiments, though the dominating sentiment is maintained by the author to be *Santi Rasa* or Quietism. The hero is King *Viveka* or Discrimination, and his Queen is *Sumati* or Wisdom. In their purpose to free the *Purusha* or Soul from the bondage of Karma, these are opposed by the whole set of passions, of which *Mahamoha* or Deep Ignorance is the head. The latter is supported by *Kama* (Love), *Krodha*, (Anger), *Darpa* (Pride), *Dambha* (Vanity), and so on. In Act I, after the prologue, Kama and his followers are introduced and some of the finest verses of our author describe his vauntings and threats against the Purusha. Then Viveka enters, and gives, in reply to the questions of his wife, a statement of purposes and procedure in liberating Purusha. In Act II, the author depicts a controversy on the stage in which the spiritual adviser of Viveka and a pupil of his, intended to present Sri Ramanuja and our author respectively, discuss the situation and are confronted with opponents of various schools whom they dispose of by argumentation, easily enough. In Acts III and IV, the characters Attachment, Hate, Jealousy, etc., are introduced and their activity among men is detailed. In Act V, Pride surveys the world 'from China to Peru' and finds no spot on earth where he is not in favour. We have here many humorous passages-at-arms between Pride, Vanity and Deceit, and the poet has succeeded in giving a realistic touch to these abstract notions by the fecundity of his imagination and the felicity of the situations introduced. Much satirical power is displayed in these Acts in exposing the abuses of various classes of society in Northern and Southern India, and the poet must have 'laughed in his sleeves' when he made Darpa (Pride) rebuke Dambha (Vanity) thus:— "You fool, I simply abstain from kicking you on the head, out of respect for your Brahminhood. Know you not that the great Tondaimandala is my native country and the famous suburb of Little Kanchi is my place of residence. The head of my family is (daily) adored by King *Skanda* and I am famous for the number of my *Sishyas* (pupils or followers) all over the world. You dispicable, old frog-in-the-well,* you alone are ignorant of my powers of irresistible argument and have probably neither seen nor heard of Me." It may be surmised that the 'Skanda Bhupala' of this passage refers to some lingering Pallava Chief who continued to live in Kanchi, after the Pallava power had been

* A well-known Indian epithet applied to an ignorant stay-at-home boor, unaware of the outside world and its news.

crushed by the Cholas; for 'Skandavarman' is a frequent name in the dynastic list of that family. In another place, our author makes Dambha (Vanity) say that he visited the precincts of the residence of Brahma in the Satyaloka, when the Great Creator rushed out of his palace to receive him, and, after washing duly his own hands seven times to remove all possible impurity, procured himself the *arghya* water, as a mark of deep respect. The reference to the frequent washing of the hands is a satiric touch that will come home to most people acquainted with Vaishnavas, who have carried ceremonial purity to the length of a science. The Act ends with a humorous description of the noon-day sun in words that compare him to a glutton flying from one pleasure to another and are appropriately put in the mouth of a follower of Mahamoha, the counterfoil to King Viveka.

In Act VI, is described an ærial voyage of King Viveka and his charioteer 'Reason' when all India is surveyed and places of interest to the Vaishnavite pilgrim are depicted. The object of the party was to seek out a quiet place for *samadhi* or meditation, and the perfectly sane conclusion is reached that, after all, surroundings are secondary, and the real seat of contemplation is one's own heart, wherever one may live, the seat of one's moral and religious sense and the abode of the Supreme Self. In Act VII, Viveka strives to fix the wandering thoughts of his charge, the Purusha, on some definite form of the Deity, to help concentration and secure victory over his enemies.

Act VIII, describes a stage-warfare between the party of Viveka and the opposite party, and concludes with the final victory of the former. The Purusha now undisturbed by conflict enters on meditation (Act IX) and finally, with the help of Vishnu-Bhakti or devotion to Vishnu surrenders himself to God and obtains final liberation (Act X). Thus King Viveka accomplishes fully the purpose that he set before himself. The Author concludes in the happiest style of his later days with a prayer that the Great Vasudeva may accept his work as He is the real author of the play and the Audience for the same.

To return to Vedanta Desika; after years of simple and retired life spent in instructing his followers, and occasional tours to sacred shrines, Vedanta Desika closed his career about 1369 A.D., having lived the full life of a hundred years and a little more, with vigour and activity. He left a son, Varadacharya by name, who became a great teacher and was the author of various works, and a sanyasin disciple, Brahma Tantra Swatantra Jiyar, who became an equally famous man and is considered to be the founder of the Parakala Mutt at Mysore. Vedanta Desika's further descendants are not known to fame, but this able writer and teacher lives in his works and is further worshipped in images in all the principal Vishnu shrines of South India, with an assiduity which will perhaps bear greater fruit if used in the study of his voluminous and edifying works.

An event, of great importance to South India

politically, occurred during Vedanta Desika's life, which we have purposely refrained from referring to till now, and which requires a brief mention, before we conclude. About 1310 A.D., Malik Kafur, a General of the Delhi Emperor Alaudin, undertook an invasion into the Dekkan with a large army. He speedily reduced the kingdoms of Warrangal and Dwarasamudra, and pushed south up to the extremity of the Peninsula, spreading devastation, and plundering everywhere. In 1312 or according to some accounts, 1326 A.D., an army of Muhammadans invaded Srirangam and pillaged the temple and city. The Vaishnavas of the city anticipated this, however, and removed the copper image of the Deity to Madura, just in time to save it from spoliation. The conquering army massacred a large number (12,000, according to one account) of Vaishnavas, and left the place in ruins. The inner shrine of the temple had however been blocked up from view, and so, it is said, escaped destruction. From this time for a period of nearly forty years, the districts of Trichinopoly and Madura, were under the rule of Muhammadan Deputies, subject to the Delhi Emperor. About 1351 A.D., the Vijianagar King Bukka I, having established a stable Hindu kingdom on the banks of the Tungabhadra, commenced to conquer the southern portions of the country recently occupied by Muhammadan Generals. He succeeded through Kampanna Odayar, his son and General, in conquering the greater part of the southern country and bringing it under Vijianagar rule. Kampanna, who established himself at Madura, was greatly assisted, in his wars by one Gopannarya, a Brahmin and a warrior. Gopanna was the Governor of Gingee, in North Arcot, which had fallen into the hands of the Vijianagar Dynasty. We have stated above that about 1326 A.D., the idol of the Srirangam God had to be taken out to Madura to escape the fury of the Muhammadan invaders. The God was gradually taken to Tirupati and worshipped duly there. When Kampanna completed his conquests in the south, Gopanna, who was no doubt a devout Vaishnavite, thought it a suitable opportunity to restore the idol to Srirangam. He brought it out from Tirupati and kept it at Gingee for a time. He then took it to Srirangam and restored it to its proper place in the shrine and directed the usual festival (which had ceased) to be commenced in connection with the idol. This fact is recorded in an inscription on the eastern wall of the temple in the form of two Sanskrit slokas,* of nearly identical meaning and the verses are preceded by the chronogram "*Bandhupriye Sakabde*" which means "In the Saka year 1293," *i.e.*, A.D., 1371. A tamil work Kovilolugu is responsible for the details of the account, and the same is also mentioned, without dates, in the Tamil Vadagali Guruparampara, as it is called, a work of about the end of the fifteenth century, which we have largely utilised in our articles. Vedanta Desika, it would seem, escaped the general massacre, being hidden by a mass of dead bodies, and betook himself with his

* *Vide* Epigraphica Indica, Vol. VI, p. 330.

followers to Mysore. He spent several years there and then went to Satyamangalam in Coimbatore. Here, in sore grief at his separation from the precincts of Srirangam, he composed the hymn *Abhiti-Stava* or 'the hymn to expel danger.' He makes reference in this work to the invasion of Muhammadans and to the cessation of worship at Srirangam, and lamenting over this great grief of his in his old age when "his head has become fully grey," prays to God to expel his enemies and return to his seat. In due time he heard, we are told, of the conquests of Gopanna and the return of the God, and himself hurried to Srirangam to enjoy the happy turn of the tide in favour of the Hindus. It is said that the first of the verses inscribed on the wall was composed by him. The Guruparampara above-mentioned further narrates that Desika lived some years after this event, built or repaired the Chidambaram Govindaraja Temple with the help of Gopanarya referred to already, and, composed the Rahasyatrayasara mentioned already, and certain other works, and finally died in the *Kartikai* month of the year *Soumya* which corresponds to November, 1369, A.D. The correctness of the last date is vouched for by other accounts, also of a traditional nature, and could not be disputed.

It will be seen that in the above account the date of Saka year 1293 or 1371 A. D., for the actual restoration of the idol to Srirangam does not fit in. for if Desika died in 1369, he could not compose the verse of the inscription in 1371. This is a discrepancy which has to be got over. Dr. Hultzsch in the "Epigraphica Indica" (Vol. vi. p. 323) points out another difficulty. It is that if Vedanta Desika lived in 1371, he could not have been born in 1269, in the Sukla year as stated in the Guruparampara; for according to him a life of 100 years and more is a great improbability and the date of birth must therefore, he says, be 'a pure invention.' This is perhaps a small matter. We have reason to think that the age of 100 years and upwards is not necessarily false, as exceptional people in those times, as well as now, lived long. Their spare diet, pure habits and high intellectuality seem to have prolonged their lives, as otherwise many reliable accounts, some of them almost contemporary, have to be treated as spurious. But even supposing that Vedanta Desika was born a couple of decades later, there is a great agreement in all accounts that he lived only up to 1369 A. D., and hence, he could not have lived to see the restoration if it really took place in 1371. Therefore, we may conclude that the story of his authorship of the verse is apocryphal and must be rejected. But there is a difficulty. If the restoration of the God was in the time of Varadachariar, Vedanta Desika's son, there was no special motive, as far as we could see, in anticipating it, as the account does not in any way connect Desika with the actual achievement of the restoration, except perhaps to show that his prayer had immediate effect. We would therefore suggest that the actual restoration of the idol was some years before the death of Vedanta Desika in 1369 A.D., say

7

about 1364 or 1365. There is nothing improbable in this, as Kampanna's activities by way of conquest commenced in 1361-62, (p. 325 vi. Epigraphica Indica) and he is said to have made some repairs at Srirangam, so that the inscription may have been engraved on the wall on the date mentioned, the actual restoration and consecration having occurred a few years before. The inscription barely recording two verses of identical meaning with a date in chronogram prefixed to them, does not look as if it was put up under the superintendence of Gopannà or of the authorities of the temple for the purpose of celebrating the restoration. We miss the full commencement, usual in inscriptions, expressing the cyclic year, month, and day of the event, intended to be recorded; and the purposeless repetition of the same facts in two successive verses, seems to justify the conclusion that memorial verses already in existence were simply engraved in an unauthorised manner with the date of engraving prefixed by the sculptor. No doubt, it may be said that the Kovilolugu account goes into great detail and gives the same date, Saka 1293. We reply that that narrative is simply a late reproduction of the apparent purport of the inscriptions and that it is inaccurate in at least two particulars, one being the *date* of the invasion where it errs by about 100 years as pointed out in the foot-note, and the other, that Saka 1293, whether taken as current or expired, cannot correspond, under any circumstances, to the 17th *Vikasi* (Solar) of the year *Paritapi*, as stated in the Kovilolugu and in some later account evidently based upon it. We have Professor Kielhorn's authority that the 2nd *tithi* of the bright half of the month Chaitra of the year Paritapi corresponded to the 7th March 1372 A.D, and was in Saka samvat 1294 expired.* Hence it is impossible to rely on the year Paritapi or even the previous year, Virodhikrit, which would correspond to Saka 1293 expired, as the date of the actual return of the idol to Srirangam. It should also be noted that, according to the verses, the victory over the *Turushkas* was after the bringing of the God to Gingee, which might have taken place any time after 1361 A.D., when Kampanna's activities in the south seem to have commenced or even before that date. We are, therefore, probably nearer the truth in conjecturing that Desika returned to Srirangam soon after the restoration of the idol, in about 1364 or 1365 A.D., and lived a few more years only, *i.e.*, till November 1369 or the year Soumya, the year of his death as preserved in the Guru Parampara Prabhava, the work of the third Brahma Tantra Jiyar, probably not much later than the end of the fifteenth century.

In confirmation of an earlier date than 1371, herein suggested for the actual restoration of the idol to Srirangam, we would also refer to the '*Yatindrapravana Vaibhavam*' of Pillai Lokarya Jiyar, Madras Edition, 1907, at p. 25 where the events stated above are also narrated and the Verse I of the inscription is quoted as composed by an '*Abhiyukta*' evidently re-

* See No. 15 of the list of inscriptions at p. 326 of E.I. Vol. vi

ferring to Vedanta Desika. The writer then states that the restoration was in the Saka year *Bahupriye*, which is a chronogram for 1283 Saka or 1361, A.D. If this is the correct reading and not *Bandhupriye* as the inscription has it, the date of the composition of this Verse and that of the restoration must be that year, rather than the later years 1364 or 1365, as suggested in the preceding paragraphs. As Chronograms, besides serving their purpose, were usually made to mean something appropriate, 'Bahupriya', 'beloved of the many' would be a more suitable name for the year in which such an important event took place than '*Bandhu priya*' 'loved by relations.' The tradition as to the year being 'Paritapi' is however repeated in this work also, a year which does not fit in with any suggested Saka year, as we have explained already, but was about the date of Malik Kafur's invasion, which may have been the cause of the confusion.

Manavala Maha Muni.

AMONG the younger contemporaries of Ramanuja Charya, mention has been made already of Parasara Bhatta, son of Kuresa, as a learned scholar and author. Born about 1074 A.D., Parasara had an exceedingly bright scholastic career, and was duly initiated in the sacred lore, by Ramanuja's cousin and pupil, Govinda. After Ramanuja's death, he became a vigorous defender of the Faith and engaged in many successful controversies. In one of these, it is said, he sought out an eminent scholar of the 'Western country' or the modern Mysore, who was a reputed Adwaitin and was, in fact, known by the name of Vedanti. It would seem that Vedanti was a rich man and usually fed hundreds of Brahmins every day. Parasara went in amongst the crowd dressed like a common man; but on reaching the inside of the house where the feast was held, approached Vedanti who was present there, and asked him to grant him the 'bhiksha' or alms of disputation. The scholar could not resist and so commenced, we are told, a controversy, for ten days, in which Parasara became the victor. He then converted Vedanti to his faith, and the latter became an important disciple. Some years after, Vedanti deserted his native country, and going to Srirangam with all that remained of his wealth, bestowed it on Parasara, and became a sanyasin under the name of '*Nanjiyar*,' 'our sanyasin,' bestowed upon him by Parasara.

The family of the Bhattars is well-known for its Sanskrit scholarship and copious contribution to the religious and philosophical literature of the day. Kuresa, the founder, has himself composed five *stotras*, on the Deities of various shrines, which are well-known for their erudition and power of expression. Two of these the *Vaikuntha Stava* and the *Atimanusha Stava*, are especially very readable and are justly favourites with Vaishnavite scholars. Parasara Bhatta has also contributed two hymns to the *stotra* literature, one on Goddess Lakshmi, who is a personality with the Vaishnavas, second only to Narayana himself. and the other on the God of Srirangam, whom Parasara looked upon almost as his father in flesh and blood. The poems are, however, rugged and not easily understandable, but the former of the hymns, the *Sriguna Ratna Kosa*, contains several stanzas of good poetry in sublime language. Among other works of this writer may be mentioned the *Tatvaratnakara* on philosophy, now partically extinct but largely quoted from by Sri Vedanta Desika, and the commentary on the Vishnu Sahasra Nama, already mentioned. Nanjiyar also composed some works, in Tamil it is to be presumed, one of which seems to have been named the *Tatwadipana*. He is better known as the author of a commentary—the 'Nine-thousands' on the Tiruvoymozhi, so-called as the quantity of syllables in the work is computed to be Nine-thousand *Granthas*, a grantha being equivalent to 32 syllables or an *anushtubh* verse. It has become usual to adopt this mode of computation in Sanskrit and Tamil works even when they are in prose, on the analogy of the Mahabharata, the Ramayana, and the Puranas, whose *grantha* computations are carefully preserved in the Colophons.

It is now proper to mention that, during this period, the study of the last named work of St. Satagopa received considerable attention from the Vaishnava scholars of the day. Specialisation was adopted and while one set of scholars continued to expound and comment upon the Sribhashya and the allied Sanskrit works, another set took to the study of the Tamil works of the Alwars, which gave them full employment. These Tamil hymns, not being argumentative treatises but merely the devotional songs of various pious men of all castes and creeds (one of them was a Pariah), poured fourth out of love and deep faith, and being couched in language which is often ancient and abstruse, lent themselves to ample comments; and the Vaishnava scholars, many of whom were good Sanskritists as well, lost no time in writing learned commentaries on the different portions of them.

Nanjiyar was succeeded by a disciple *Kalivairi* or *Nampillai*, who taught the Tamil hymns largely and composed a commentary on a small portion out of them. A disciple of Nampillai, Vadakku-Tiru-Vedhi-Pillai by name, is the author of an extensive commentary known as the 'Thirty-six-Thousand.' This work is an inexhaustible storehouse of traditions on the different interpretations of the text and gives us a good idea of the amount of industry and learning that was brought to bear on the study of these Tamil works. Periavachchan Pillai was another of Nampillai's pupils who wrote full commentaries, on the Tiruvoymozhi and the other hymns as well and was a most prolific and well-informed writer of the day. As is inevitable, differences of views arose on points of construction as well as on details of doctrine between the above set of writers who came to be called the Southern School or the Tengalais and the writers of the Northern School, generally known as the Vadagalais, who, though more largely patronising Sanskrit works, had still an equal regard for the Tamil hymns and expounded them in their lectures. Vedanta Desika himself, as representing the latter class, was, as we have seen, an able Tamil scholar and author and is said to have composed a commentary on the Tiruvoymozhi, which is not now extant. But various authors after his date have written such commentaries and at least 5 exist now, which are studied by various sections of the orthodox Vadagalai class.

To the next generation of writers belonged Pillai Loka Charya, son of the author of the 'Thirty-six-Thousand' commentary, but a pupil of Nampillai and author of various works in Sanskritised Tamil, the most important of these are the *Sri Vachana Bhushana* and the *Tatwa Traya*. These works are in terse and elliptic style and were evidently meant as summaries in pithy language of doctrines which were expounded orally at great length. Pillay Loka Charya was an elderly contemporary of Sri Vedanta Desika; and the latter, in his works, especially, the *Rahasyatraya Sura*, alludes in various places to his views and purports to controvert them. The *Tatwatraya* is an exposition of the principles of the Visistadwaita philosophy and its view of the development of the universe and the inter-relationship of the souls and God. The other work, the *Vachana Bhushana*, is held in extraordinary veneration by the followers of this school, as a repository of secret and esoteric doctrines, incapable of being understood except under the direct teaching of a duly qualified preceptor. The chief features of the book are the doctrine of surrender to one's *Acharya* or Guru, advocated by this writer as a sufficient means of salvation, the emphasis given to the doctrine of Grace by the assertion that even the sins of men are agreeable to God, and the somewhat unceremonious rejection of caste-superiority as a ground for respect among men otherwise equally venerable as lovers of God. It will be perceived that the last is a feature which must ensure the adherence of non-Brahmin Vaishnavites generally, who form a majority among those of the Southern School. The excessive adoration of the Guru, as yet theoretical in Southern India, has become, as we shall see, a permanent feature of Northern Vaishnavaism as developed by Ramanand and his followers, who also, from the necessities of their position, threw all caste distinctions to the winds, and drew followers from every class and creed.

The next writer of note in this school of Vaishnavas was the well-known Manavala Maha Muni, whose name has been appropriated for the heading of this paper. He was born near Alwar-Tirunagari about 1370 A. D., and is said to have lived for 73 years, *i.e.*, up to 1443 A. D. Of well-built proportions and extremely fair, almost white, in appearance, he soon attracted attention by his intelligence and ability and came to be recognised as an eminent scholar. He was a pupil of one Sri Sailesa or *Tiruvoymozhi Pillai*, a teacher of the Tamil hymns, as the name implies. He spent his early years at Tirunagari and then moved to Srirangam, the holy city of so many eminent divines. Here he permanently established himself and acquired a large following of pupils and admirers. His life's work was partly composition and instruction, and partly the systematic organization of his followers under various centres or Sees, the acquiring of control over temple management and ritual in various places, and the repair of shrines in various districts out of funds collected from the richer of his followers or paid voluntarily by devotees.

Among other works, Manavala has composed commentaries on the two works of Pillai Loka Charya mentioned already. His commentaries are characterised by great clearness and fulness of exposition. He possesses the great merit, found in few other Hindu writers of giving references to the quotations spread throughout important Tamil works like the 'Thirty-six Thousands' commentary, and always quotes the sources of the texts that he himself extracts. His range of studies must have been large and he was an eminent scholar in Sanskrit and Tamil. His original works are, however, few; in fact only three or four are known to posterity. One of them is the *Yatirajavimsati* or twenty verses in Sanskrit in praise of Sri Ramanuja, and is in simple style. We find here the curious introduction of initial rhyme in many of the stanzas; that is to say, the second syllables of the four lines of each verse are identical, a feature universal in Tamil prosody but unknown to Sanskrit readers; though final rhyme, as in English poetry, is occasionally met with in Sanskrit.* The other works, the *Upadesaratnamala* and the *Arthiprabandha* are in Tamil verse. The former is a list of the names of Alwars and chief teachers with some account of their works. The latter is a passionate appeal to Sri Ramanuja in heaven, to end his days and liberate him from the physical ills which seem to have worried him late in life, and the torment of worldly existence which every Hindu is expected to detest. Manavala Maha Muni had a son Ramanuja who seems to have died before him and a grandson Jiyar Nayinar, who survived him. He had numerous disciples, some of them sanyasins like himself. One of the lay pupils was one Prativvadibhayamkara, who, as his name implies was a scholar of some eminence. Two of his works now exist; one, a commentary on the *Ashta Sloki* of

* See its use, with great effect, in the Ramayana, Sundara Kanda, Cantos V and VII, and in the poem '*Nalodaya*' attributed to Kalidasa, where the last five syllables of each of four lines are identical.

Parasara Bhatta, and the other a vigorous laudatory poem of 70 verses on Sri Vedanta Desika. We have clear indications in this later work of the growing dissensions between the adherents of the two schools. The author of the 70 verses asserts his indebtedness to the teachings of Vedanta Desika and his son Varadacharya (1317 to 1414 A. D.), and states that he is a pupil of the latter. It is understood however that he later became an adherent of Manavala Maha Muni. The chief disciples of Manavala, of whom the first was Vanamamalai Jeer, the founder of the Mutt of that name in the Tinnevelly district, are known by the name of 'Ashta Diggajas' or '*the eight elephants*, guarding the eight quarters' in evident allusion to the strong support which they gave to their chief in the promulgation of his doctrines.

There are various points in theory and practices in which the two schools, which are now known as the Vadagalais and Tengalais, differ; one such is the well-known distinction in the vertical caste-mark as worn in the forehead, the Vadagalais using a parabolic form, the base of which is nearly in a line with the brows, the other class using two somewhat broad straight marks slanting in opposite directons, outwards, and supported on a base which is itself a small triangle, base upwards with the vertex lower down, about the apex or in some cases the centre, of the nose. The central red streak is common to both, and is meant to represent Lakshmi. But the chief item of controversy between these two schools, which has engaged the attention of Magistrates and Judges, is the claim of either sect to officiate exclusively in the temple rituals and worship, to the accompaniment of certain recitations commencing with what has come to be known as the *patrams*. The recitation of the Tamil songs of the Alwars has been connected with temple ritual from the time of Ramanuja, and possibly from earlier times also. The *patram* is however, for each community, a single stanza in *anushtubh-metre*, which sets forth the name of its leading Teacher, and is peculiar to him. The one used by the Vadagalai community commences with the words '*Ramanuja-daya-patram*,' meaning 'recipient of the kindness (*i.e.* teachings) of Ramanuja,' the Ramanuja referred to here being the Atreya Ramanuja, uncle of Vedanta Desika and his immediate teacher. The other verse is on the same plan but has for its first words *Srisailesa*, the teacher of Manavala and refers to the latter as his pupil. There is nothing in the verse of either party to wound the susceptibilities of the followers of the other; but of course the right of commencement is fought out eagerly, as it is the prelude to the exercise of other rights in the temple and neither party is willing to use or listen to the recital of the other's verse, as it may imply an allegiance which it stoutly refuses to grant. The English educated community of either sect and those among the others who have no chances of participating in temple emoluments have no relish for such unseemly disputes, and regard them as deplorable. It is to be hoped that, as education increases and the spirit of national life develops, the two sects may learn greater toleration and manage to live in peace, studying the works of their teachers, instead of getting them up parrot-like, and engaging in free-fights on such trivial matters as the *patrams*.

Sree Chaitanya.

THE development of Vaishnavaism has now been traced, though only in the form of sketches of the lives of the principal exponents, from the earliest times to about the middle of the Fifteenth Century. In South India it is clear that from the early years of the Christian era, this cult flourished under the strong impetus given by the Alwars, who by their Tamil songs, inculcated Bhakti and Krishna-worship mainly. The Alwars were saints or *Bhaktas* of various castes, who were unique in their devotion to God, and led lives remarkable for their religious fervour and difference to worldly pleasures. Three early Alwars named respectively the *Poykai Alwar*, the *Bhutathalwar*, and the *Peyalwar* were mythical in their origin and are said to have met at the modern Tirukkoilur, where they had a vision of God and poured forth their joy at the sight, in Tamil verses of a hundred each. These Alwars speak of Narayana as the highest God, allude frequently to the early Avatars of Vishnu especially the Tiruvikrama or the Vamana and are eloquent in their admiration of the Krishna-Avatar. They presuppose the chief Puranas and are anterior to all the rest of the Alwars. They adore the idols of the more ancient shrines of South India, like those at Srirangam, Tirupati, Alagarkoil, etc. They speak with respect of Vedic lore, but teach the worship of the Deity by recitations of His names, services at the temples and contemplation of his personal forms. *Tirumalisai Alwar* was the next in order of time and he has composed about 200 stanzas. Of the later Alwar, Saint Satagopa or *Nammalwar* has been mentioned already more than once in these pages. Of the rest Vishnuchitta or *Perialwar*, *Kulasekaralwar*, who was a ruler of ancient Travancore, and *Tirumangai Alwar* are the most noted and have composed extensive songs. The list of Alwars included a lady, *Andal*, daughter of Vishnuchitta; a pariah devotee, *Tiruppanalwar*, who has composed but 10 stanzas, and a pupil of Nammalwar, *Madhurakavi* who was a worshipper of his Guru, exclusively. We find nowhere among these Alwars any denunciation of Brahmins as such or protests against the caste system; they represent in no sense any rise of the lower castes against the Brahmin Priesthood and the frequent denunciations of Budhists and Jains show who their contemporaries were. It seems reasonable to conclude that these Alwars or the earlier of them were the offshoots of the Northern Bhagavatas or Vaishnavites and that they devoted their lives to pious worship of the personal forms of God, and visits to the shrines of Vishnu. The Bhagavad-Gita was well known to them and the Bhagavata in some form also, for their works are saturated with Sri Krishna's early life and its miraculous incidents.

The Acharyas from Nathamnni downwards form the next phase of development in the Vaishnava faith, and represent the intellectual, as the Alwars do the emotional side. A construction of Philosophy which was fit to be placed before the best intellect of the land and which at the same time gave room for the absorption of the teachings of the Alwars and the doctrine of Bhakti, was the chief feature of this work. Caste was firmly supported, all heresy was eschewed and the shastras were fully upheld by these Acharyas, while at the same time purity of life, superiority of devotion, and fervid adoration of Narayana in his Avatars and idol manifestations were also inculcated. Ramanuja represents the climax of these teachings and in him we have the philosopher and the devotee happily combined. The philosophy is healthy and sympathetic, the devotion has not degenerated to fanaticism or irrational worship. The doctrine of *Prapatti* or Surrender was inculcated to suit inferior intellects. Ramanuja in no place countenances the slightest departure from strict Shastraic injunction. He is uncompromising in denying the privilege of Vedic study to Sudras and women and the latter were never permitted to mix with men in devotion or abandon their usual household duties much less to assume the character of nuns. *Bhajanas*, *Sankirtans*, festive songs, etc., were practically unheard of in those days and religious fervour never took the form of violent demonstrations or indecent exhibitions.

In the centuries following that in which Ramanuja lived, *i.e.*, the twelfth and the two succeeding centuries these features of Vaishnavaism were greatly preserved.

Non-Brahmin adherents no doubt increased in number but we hear nowhere of the protest against the caste restriction and the assertion of general equality which is a permanent feature of modern Vaishnavaism as seen in the North. It must be admitted however that the germs of these doctrines began to be visible about the beginning of the Fifteenth Century in the preachings of certain of the Vaishnavaite teachers in Southern India. We have alluded in the life of Manavala Maha Muni to the emphasis given to the spiritual equality of the Brahmin and the Sudra *Bhakta* and the assertion of the doctrine that the Guru was the ultimate Saviour. A curious mode of expressing the difference of views in the operation of God's grace was this: some asserted that divine grace acted *like the monkey*, *i.e.*, the souls must exert themselves to get saved, as the young of the monkey actively seizes its mother during the latter's evolutions from tree to tree. Others more indolent or more hopeful according as one may view it, asserted that God's grace was *like the cat*, which safeguarded its young, unaided by any efforts of the latter. God's graces according to this latter school, was irresistible and required nothing but an attitude of recaptivity to freely flow to the deepest sinner. Hence the maxim, "fatal to many Hindu sects" as Barth points out, 'that the acts of the true devotee, of the Bhakta, are indifferent, and that the man who has once experienced the effects of Grace, whatever he may do, can sin no longer.' Such doctrines, carried to their logical conclusions, dangerously minimise responsibility and beget a familiarity with sin, and an audacious disregard of purity in life.

Another doctrine equally fatal to progress was the Guru-worship or deification of the immediate preceptor. With regard to the founders of the various systems, there may be some justification for ascribing to them divine origin and powers. But the deification of every later Guru, however theoretically disciplinary it may be, to the pupil, is largely destructive of rational thought and the spirit of self-reliance, and encourages superstitious veneration for persons who may have lost all claim for respect.

It is to the above causes that we must ascribe the degeneration of Vaishnavaism in Northern India, in later days. In the South, doctrines like those mentioned above found little practical support and never led to the levelling of the castes or the adoption of questionable habits. The grip of the Shastra and established social rules, was too strong to be shaken by the Brahmin Vaishnavites, and the Sudra followers were generally inferior in importance and never asserted themselves. Any show of equality by the higher castes was valued as a privilege and the respect for the Brahmin as Brahmin, born in the flesh from Manu's days, was never forgotten. The comparative political quiet of the South also contributed to preserve the higher castes from disruption or admixture with the lower. But in the North, Vaishnavaism first affected the lower strata of society and proceeded upwards in its conversions. In Bengal, Saktaism had taken deep root among the Brahmins who practised their horrible mystic rites in secret and excluded the lower castes. In Benares and Western India, the Brahmins were generally enlightened advaitees to whom the cult of devotion and faith had no attractions. Hence the first converts to Vaishnavaism were there also the lower castes. It was therefore inevitable that the habits and customs of the converts should react on the religion newly adopted and present phases of it which are alike strange and inexplicable to the earlier adherents of the same faith in the South.

It is perhaps not quite true that all the Vaishnavaism found in the North was imported from the South after Ramanuja's days. The land of Krishna's birth, overrun as it was by frequent devastating armies, was still a place of resort to vast crowds as a holy centre. And the Krishna cult that had taken such a deep root there in the early centuries of the Christian era, was not altogether without power during the intervening centuries. But any how its potency was slumbering and before it shone forth again, it had to be fanned anew by a fresh breeze of Vaishnavaism from the Southern lands, where it was thriving, thanks to the Alwars and Acharyas who had sedulously fostered it.

The chief Vaishnavites of Northern India are the Ramanandis, the Vallabacharis, and the Chaitanyas. Ramanand, the founder of the first of these sects, is said to have been the fifth in apostolic succession from Ramanuja and to have lived in the end of the fourteenth century. There is nothing improbable in the story usually given that Ramanand, insulted by Vaishnavites of the South among whom he lived, for his social inferiority, travelled north and established a Mutt at Benares and had numerous followers. He advocated the doctrine of Bhakti of course, asserted the supreme efficacy of the *Rama* mantra, and discarded social distinctions. It may be mentioned that Rama-worship as distinguiseed from that of Krishna is unknown in the South, and it is therefore incorrect to say, as some writers do, that Ramanuja inculcated Rama-worship. A pupil of Ramanand or one of his successors, Nabhaji by name, wrote the *Bhaktamala* or the lives of saints which is practically the scripture of the Ramanandis. The famous Tulsidas (1532—1623 A.D.) seventh in descent from Ramanand, "one of the greatest reformers and one of the greatest poets that India has produced," in the opinion of Dr. Grierson, is the author of the Hindi Ramayana, which is a text-book of religious philosophy for millions in Upper India. The pupils of Ramanand are from various lower castes. One of them was a Muhammadan weaver named Kabir and he founded a system whose object was to amalgamate Hindus and Muhammadans. Rama was the god of worship; but forms and *mantras* were excluded. When Kabir died his corpse was claimed by both sects and the remains, miraculously converted to flowers, were shared by Hindus and Muhammadans. Nanak carried out the same purpose of reconciliation of Hindus and Muhammadans in the Punjab and gave rise to the *Sikh* clans, literally *sishyas.* Sikkism has been described as Muhammadanism *minus* circumcision and cow-killing and *plus* faith in the divinity of the Gurus. It is said that Sikkism is now on the wane and is being absorbed into some form of Hinduism. The *Adi Granth,* the Bible of the Sikhs, contains Hindu doctrines and is worshipped as a *divinity* by itself.

The other two sects of Vaishnavaism and their innumerable sub-sects are all founded on the worship of Krishna. In the Vallabha religion, *Balagopala,* the child Krishna gorgeously dressed, is the object of worship. The Bhagavata is the foundation of the Krishna Leela or the early exploits of Krishna. Krishna is worshipped along with or in conjunction with the Gopis; but *Radha,* the unmarried consort of Krishna, is not usually associated with him.

Vallabhacharya, the founder of this sect or at least its most famous exponent, was born about 1749 A. D., in Telingana and settled at Muttra to teach his doctrines. The worship of Krishna and the indulgence in the rhapsodies of the Bhagavata and the Gita Govinda tended to increase luxury and licentiousness in the Maharajahs or High Priests of this sect and its followers. The worst forms of sexual love and immorality became tolerated and commended as religious. Many of the immoralities of this rich and highly influential sect were exposed in a case which went up to the Supreme Court of Bombay in 1862.

The Chaitanyas who now remain to be described are most general in Bengal. They are now branched into various sects, some of them made up of the richer and the higher classes while the majority seem to be of the lowest classes, containing the worst dregs of the population. The special feature of this sect was the adoption of *Radha Krishna*, as the object of worship. Jayadeva's *Gita-Govinda* mentioned already gives a good idea of the influence which the erotic sentiment commenced to exercise on Hindus even so early as the 12th Century. The most commendable attitude of the soul to God was represented by the position of the beloved to her lover. Married love was considered of a lower form, being interested; the love towards the gallant, subversive of worldly duty and propriety as it was, was considered the highest kind of sentiment that the soul can entertain towards the Almighty. Radha-worship was inculcated by Chaitanya in the beginning of the 16th Century. But there is reason to think that this kind of worship is as ancient as the beginning of the Christian era, if not earlier. Krishna's amours had been spiritualised from the earliest times. The ardent longing of the Gopis for Krishna was considered typical of the souls' longing for God, and sages and poets who cannot be suspected of favouring moral lapses have agreed to regard the Krishna Idylls as symbolic of the highest spiritual devotion that is possible to man. Many of Nammalwar's hymns and those of other saints in the Tamil land typify this phase of devotion, and other religions have adopted the ideal of female love as typical of adoration due to the Most High. However this may be, the chief popularity of the Radha cult arose, of course, from the full play it gave to the amorous side of human nature. In the earlier stages and in the case of those adherents who were morally strong, there is no doubt it led to no excess or abuse. But human nature of the yielding type which it generally is, can hardly resist long the insinuations to moral fall which such excessive hankerings are bound to produce, and it is therefore no wonder that the Radha Krishna devotion, and the promiscuous mingling of the sexes which it permitted, have degraded to a pitiful degree vast crowds of Chaitanya Vaishnavites whose ignorance and superstition give them no chance of reformation. Many of the Chaitanya sects adopted the reprehensible practices of the Tantrics or Saktas and hence fell into those very sins which moved the moral wrath of Chaitanya and prompted his attempts at reform.

It was in the city of Navadwip or Nuddea on the Ganges that the boy Nimai or Visvambhara, the future Chaitanya, was born about 1485 A.D. His father Jaganath Misra was a high-caste Brahmin and an immigrant into Nuddea from Sylhet. He married Saachee, daughter of Nilambar, a learned man of Nuddea. Nuddea was then, as it has been ever since, the home of the Nyaya philosophy; and Pundit Sarvabhauma was teaching subtle syllogisms there during the early years of Visvambhara's life. Visvarupa, the elder brother of Visvambhara was Sarvabhauma's pupil. While yet a boy, Visvarupa suddenly left home and resolved to become an ascetic. He wandered over many places, finally settled at Pandharpur in Western India, and seems to have died there. There are however some mysterious hints in Chaitanya's lives, that Visvarupa was identical with the ascetic friend and constant companion, Nityananda of Chaitanya. But the better opinion seems to be that the two are different.

Visvambhara's early life was frolicsome, michievous, and worrying to his parents in a high degree. He became a spoilt child and freely indulged in his whims, one of which was frequent weeping and dancing. About the ninth year he was invested with the sacred thread, and he then went to attend the *tole* of Gangadas, a pandit of the place. There he studied Grammar, and, it is said, acquired great proficiency in it. He then attended the Nyaya College of Sarvabhauma, where he came in contact with several advanced pupils who, later, became his companions. One of these was Raghunath, the author of the commentary *Didhiti* on the *Chintamani*, the modern text-book of Nyaya. We are assured by the author of 'Lord Gauranga,' that Visvambhar himself wrote such a subtle work on logic, that it excited the fear and wonder of Raghunath and that the former thereupon tore it to pieces to please Raghunath who was ambitious to be unrivalled. It is perhaps likely that Visvambhara did not obtain any great proficiency under Sarvabhauma, if he read under him at all. It is certain that Sarvabhauma, whom Visvambhara met some years after, did not recognise in him, a former pupil of any eminence. He simply recognised Chaitanya as the son of his former friend and companion, Jagannatha. Then

Visvambhara started a grammar school of his own at the early age of sixteen and attracted followers and pupils. He was now married to one Lakshmi, daughter of a Vallabhacharya, but the lady died 2 or 3 years after marriage. He then married again Vishnupriya, a girl of great gentleness of character and devotion to Chaitanya.

Visvambhara was now about 20 years of age. He had been initiated into the Vaishnavite faith by one Isvarapuri, a pious devotee. He now undertook a trip to Gaya, the holy place. The sight of Vishnu's foot-prints there produced a wonderful change in his sensitive nature. He lost himself in frequent thought and yearned deeply for a sight of Sri Krishna. Here he again met Iswarapuri and the contact of the ascetic made him long for Krishna the more. He was taken back by his friends to Nuddea and tried to commence his school work. But this was found impossible and he had to give it up entirely. He found himself constantly talking of Sri Krishna and the Gopis, the Brindavan and its attractions; and the impossibility of life under normal conditions became apparent. He became subject to trances and visions, and, more than once, seemed to have attained to the presence of Krishna. The friends and followers of Sri Chaitanya who have recorded the details of his life in various works in Sanskrit and Bengali, feel no doubt whatever that in these days Visvambhara's body was subjected to a spiritual pervasion by Sri Krishna himself. During these moments when the Lord came upon him, he was not Visvambhara at all. In his ordinary moods he danced and sang and was delirious with *Bhakti* or devotion. He imagined himself to be Radha and acted her part to perfection. But when he was overpowered by Krishna's *Avesa*, he knew not what he did. He was a medium and the followers perceived only Sri Krishna and his miraculous doings. Thus on one occasion he entered the puja house of an elderly friend *Srivas*, a wealthy householder, and taking his seat on the *dais* reserved for the idols, called out in tones of command that "He had come," and wanted *Abishekam* or the sacred bath. He was duly bathed, dressed and worshipped. All around fell at his feet and were rewarded with gracious replies. The *seance* lasted several hours and then Nimai fell down in a swoon. When he awoke he was dumbfounded at the situation and recollected nothing. At another time his friend Nityananda beheld his beauteous form, expanded into large proportions, with six hands, two of which bore the bow and arrows like Rama, and two others were playing on the flute like Krishna, while the remaining two held the staff and the waterpot, typical of his future sanyasin's state. It may be added that the typical figure of Chaitanya or Gouranga in the numerous places where he is worshipped, is the six-headed figure, the body representing on the right Sri Krishna and the left Radha. Nityananda is devoutly believed to be Balarama himself, elder brother of Sri Krishna, whose avatar was Visvambhara himself.

A most important follower acquired in these days

by the future Chaitanya was Adwaitacharya, an elderly Vaishnavite pundit and scholar. He had frequent opportunities of seeing Visvambhara in his trances and had vision of him as Sri Krishna. His cultivated mind, however doubted, and it was reserved to Visvambhara in one of his moods, to proceed to his village Santipur, some miles down the Ganges, from Nuddea, and *literally* beat the truth of his divine nature into the head of Adwaita. The holy man, it is said, took the chastisement as a most pleasurable exercise and was duly and thoroughly cured of his lingering scepticism! Another miracle which Gauranga achieved was the conversion of the brothers, Jagannath and Madhava, two notorious sinners, who had great influence in Nuddea and whom Gouranga openly humbled. It is said that he took upon himself their hideous sins and saved them completely. Gouranga brought about a dramatic representation at the residence of one Chandrasekhar, a relative of his, in which Adwaita played the part of Sri Krishna, Gouranga himself that of Radha and Sri Vas, that of Narada. The subject of the play was the meeting of Radha and Krishna in the Brindavan and the characters were Krishna, and his friends and Gopees. In this representation, we are told the various characters represented, entered spiritually the bodies of the respective actors and the play was really a grim reality, in which Krishna's early life was re-enacted.

A most important change in Visvambhar's life now occurred. This was nothing less than his renunciation of worldly life and initiation as sanyasin under the name of Sri Krishna Chaitanya, his future designation. The initiation was by one Kesava Bharati, an ascetic who lived at a village some 18 miles from Nuddea and to whom Nimai went up in great secrecy, having given the slip to his friends and family. His friends and relations however traced him but were unable to impede his progress to sanyasinhood. Chaitanya himself considered his ordination as the *summum bonum* of his life and an inexpressible joy and Krishna-madness seized him at once. For three days he wandered about thinking to reach Brindavan and spend his remaining life there. Some of his friends followed him with difficulty and brought him back to Nuddea. To the great grief of his mother, life at Nuddea was considered objectionable and it was arranged that Chaitanya should settle at Puri or Jagannath, a place not too far off and sufficiently sacred to satisfy his spiritual cravings.

To Jaganath, then, he went, accompained by a few trusted followers. Jagannath was in the dominions of Pratapa Rudra, King of Orissa, a Hindu Monarch of great power, who ruled from 1504—1532, A.D. and whose capital was Cuttack. The King's favourite Pundit and Principal of the Sanskrit College at Puri was the great logician, Sarvabhauma under whom, it has been mentioned, Chaitanya himself had read for a short time. Sarvabhauma was all in all with the temple authorities, and through his help, Gouranga and his friends had access to the innermost shrine. Chaitanya feasted his eyes on the holy image and lost himself in ecstasy. Gopinath Acharya, a brother-in-law of Sarvabhauma, was well aware of Chaitanya's greatness and divine indications and was of much use to him. In due time the great scholar Sarvabhauma himself was converted by Chaitanya and became an humble follower.

The author of "Lord Gouranga" says that there was a great Shastraic disputation between the two, and Chaitanya was completely victorious. The *Chaitanya-chandrodaya*, of Karnapura, son of Sivananda, a contemporary of Gouranga, does not mention the disputation but narrates that the conversion was the miraculous effect of God Jagannadha's 'Holy' Prasad or food-offering, which Chaitanya took to Sarvabhauma one morning and imperiously compelled him to swallow. Any how a complete conversion of Sarvabhauma to the doctrine of faith in Krishna was the result. King Pratapa Deva's conversion duly followed and Chaitanya, who was now more obviously an avatar than he had ever been before, and whose spiritual power had become irresistible, established himself at Puri and propagated his faith throughout the length and breadth of Orissa and Bengal.

Two other events in the life of Chaitanya were of great importance in extending his influence. One was his trip to South India, when he is said to have visited Vijiangar and converted one Ramanand Roy, a Brahmin official of some importance under Krishnadeva Raya. This Southern tour seems to have been a rapid but extensive one and many miracles are related in connection with it. The other event we would refer to was the visit of Chaitanya to Benares and his victory over Prakasananda, an advaita sanyasin of great scholarship who subsequently became a follower of Chaitanya under the name of Probodhananda.

After staying some dozen years at Puri, Chaitanya seems to have travelled again to Nuddea and thence to Benares and Brindavan. He made proper arrangements for the teaching of his doctrine of *Krishna-Prem* or love to Krishna. Adwaita and Nityanand were stationed to work in Bengal. Rupa and Sanatana, two other pupils, were sent to Muttra. He himself lived a strict life of religious fervour and constant devotion and finally disappeared about 1527, having converted many millions of people to the Krishna faith in Bengal and Orissa, the chief scenes of his activity.

Whatever may be the truth about Chaitanya's Divinity, it is clear that he was, in actual life, the Sri Krishna for the Sixteenth Century. Writing in 1872, Hunter, in his *Orissa*, says :—

> The adoration of Chaitanya has become a sort of family-worship throughout Orissa. In Puri, there is a temple specially dedicated to his name and many little shrines are scattered over the country. But he is generally adored in connection with Vishnu and of such joint temples there are at present 300 in the town of Puri and 500 in the districts......At this moment Chaitanya is the apostle of the common people in Orissa. The death of this reformer marks the spiritual decline of Vishnu-worship.

Chaitanya who, as Barth calls him, was perhaps all but 'a poor enthusiastic visionary,' had a few converts from Mahomedanism among his followers. It does not appear, however, that he ever preached any Mahomedan doctrine or tried to assimilate, like Kabir or Nanak, the two essentially different religions, Hinduism and Mahommedanism. *Within* the pale of Hinduism, he recognised apparently no caste distinction. He seems to have preached a mild and unobjectionable form of Krishna-worship and his personal character was attractive and highly lovable. We have absolutely no reason to suppose that, by his mode of worship, he countenanced or would have countenanced the disgraceful excesses which now characterise the lower orders among his followers, and a reckless ambition to spite his rivals and persecutors at Nuddea, by developing a counter-cult to Saktaism, does not, as has been supposed, appear to be a natural part of his character as disclosed in the extant accounts of his life. Chaitanya is said to have built many shrines at Brindavan ; and his native district of Nuddea contains, as Orissa does, many Chaitanya images under actual worship. Dr. Bhattacharya writing of the Chaitanya sect says :—

> The sect that he has founded has developed into a gigantic body which threatens to throw into shade the representatives of his old enemies, if not to make them all humble followers.

Assuming that Chaitanya was no divinity but a simple religious reformer, impelled by the strength of his devotion to proclaim his doctrines, we have in him another instance of deification so thorough and complete, that, even before he died, his image was installed for worship and the incidents of his life were modified and magnified into miracles which proved his divine nature. There is nothing strange if we remember that such has been the rule in the case of every great reformer from *Buddha* down to *Ramakrishna Paramahamsa*, the Saint of Dakshineswar, who is the most recent instance of this process of deification.